Business on the Edge

ALSO BY VIVA ONA BARTKUS

The Dynamic of Secession
Getting It Right (with Ed Conlon)
Social Capital: Reaching Out, Reaching In (with James H. Davis)

Business on the Edge

How to Turn a Profit and Improve Lives in the World's Toughest Places

Viva Ona Bartkus and Emily S. Block

BASIC BOOKS
NEW YORK

Basic Books
Hachette Book Group
1290 Avenue of the Americas, New York, NY 10104
www.basicbooks.com

Printed in the United States of America

First Edition: July 2024

Published by Basic Books, an imprint of Hachette Book Group, Inc. The Basic Books name and logo is a registered trademark of the Hachette Book Group.

Names and identifying details of individuals in frontline environments have been changed.

The Hachette Speakers Bureau provides a wide range of authors for speaking events. To find out more, go to www.hachettespeakersbureau.com or email HachetteSpeakers@hbgusa.com.

Basic books may be purchased in bulk for business, educational, or promotional use. For more information, please contact your local bookseller or the Hachette Book Group Special Markets Department at special.markets@hbgusa.com.

The publisher is not responsible for websites (or their content) that are not owned by the publisher.

Print book interior design by Sheryl Kober.

Library of Congress Cataloging-in-Publication Data

Names: Bartkus, Viva Ona, author. | Block, Emily S., author.
Title: Business on the edge : how to turn a profit and improve lives in the world's toughest places / Viva Ona Bartkus and Emily S. Block.

Description: First edition. | New York : Basic Books, 2024. | Includes bibliographical references and index.

Identifiers: LCCN 2023050039 | ISBN 9781541604209 (hardcover) | ISBN 9781541604216 (ebook)
Subjects: LCSH: Businesses--Developing countries. | Management--Developing countries.
Classification: LCC HD70.D44 B38 2024 | DDC 658.009172/4--dc23/eng/20231106
LC record available at https://lccn.loc.gov/2023050039
ISBNs: 9781541604209 (hardcover), 9781541604216 (ebook)

LSC-C

10 9 8 7 6 5 4 3 2 1

For Ava and Abigail

In loving memory of McKenna and Noah

CONTENTS

Introduction 1

PART I: THE OPPORTUNITY

Chapter 1: The Juice Is Worth the Squeeze 000

Chapter 2: Security Is Not a Fixed Cost 000

Chapter 3: Savvy Supply Chains 000

Chapter 4: Partnerships Mitigate Risk 000

PART II: THE PROCESS

Chapter 5: Follow the Money 000

Chapter 6: Partner Broadly 000

Chapter 7: Imagine and Create Common Ground 000

Chapter 8: Dirty Boots & Open Hearts 000

Chapter 9: Fail Fast & Fail Forward 000

Conclusion: Nothing Stops a Bullet Like a Job 000

Acknowledgments 000

Notes 000

Index 000

INTRODUCTION

When an artillery shell exploded nearby, fear mobilized us into action. Instinctively, we both dove for cover under the only folding table in the tent deep in the backwoods of North Carolina. We emerged moments later, pantsuits covered in dust, to the laughter of half a dozen US Special Operations officers who hadn't even flinched. After six years traveling the world as part of Business on the Frontlines (BOTFL), an MBA course exploring the role of business in rebuilding war-torn societies, we were no strangers to the sounds of gunfire in the distance. That year alone, we had served local partners in Rwanda, Sierra Leone, and Guatemala. But this was the closest we had been to an explosion. Up until this point, we had collaborated mainly with humanitarian organizations and multinational corporations, but we were intrigued by the opportunity to work with a branch of the US armed services. The incoming commander of the US Army Special Operations Command, Lieutenant General Charles Cleveland, shared our belief that increasing economic opportunity could promote stability around the world, and he invited us to meet with some of his soldiers in Fort Bragg, North Carolina (renamed Fort Liberty in 2023). Upon our arrival, we piled into a Jeep with several officers who, unbeknownst to us, had brought us onto a forward operating base (FOB in military speak) during a live-fire training exercise. Although the exploding shell posed no real danger to us, it still shook the ground and our confidence. Perhaps they did it to haze us or to test our mettle. Regardless, it felt like a rocky beginning.

Dodging artillery wasn't what we imagined we'd be doing when we set out to change how business is conducted around the world. Our work with the Business on the Frontlines program aims to harness the principles and energy of business to rebuild societies ravaged by war and poverty, which we call *frontline* environments. The frontlines exist on the edge of many of the things we take for granted: along disputed borders and distant from urban centers, where populations are stranded without support. The frontlines are on the edge of the wave of globalization, as many Western innovations and investments have stopped just short of their reach. They are on the edge of our existing business models, processes, and thinking, and they now represent the leading edge of business, able to unlock new opportunities and generate real economic returns. And they lie on the edge of business's traditional mandate. Although business has historically been left out of the peace-building and development puzzle, when done thoughtfully and in concert with cross-sector partners, it can become an integral part of imagining novel solutions to the world's thorniest problems. Our experience shows that business can turn a profit and improve lives in the frontlines. In fact, for businesses that have the will to act swiftly and the commitment to acquire new skill sets, the advantages can be tremendous.

But it will not be business as usual.

When we say "business," many people think of a *who*: a multinational corporation, a factory, or even a local street vendor. In our mind, those are *businesses*. We think of *business*, in the singular, as a *what*: a set of disciplined principles and processes that facilitate problem solving and sustainable growth.

As a mindset, business asks basic questions, starting with how to create value for the customer. This requires a product (or service) and a customer—and finding both is often surprisingly difficult, particularly in the frontlines. Take, for example, sacha inchi. A nut from the jungles of Peru and Colombia, sacha inchi's properties make it an Amazonian superfood. It has a high concentration of nutrients, with more omega-3 than herring, salmon, or mackerel. It grows quickly and can be harvested every six weeks or so. This nut is nearly indestructible, so there is almost no loss due to damage during transportation, no matter how poor the roads. In recent years, nongovernmental organizations (NGOs) have encouraged impoverished farmers to grow sacha inchi to improve their livelihoods.

Yet in rural Peru and Colombia, mounds of sacha inchi line the roadside.

Why? Frankly, sacha inchi is disgusting. It tastes like rancid fish oil, and despite its health benefits, no one wants to eat it. Perhaps in the future, food processors may develop a way to grind it into a powder, make a paste, combine it as an additive in other foods, or even douse it with chocolate to mask the taste. But presently, farmers have no business growing sacha inchi, as there is no market for it. They have the product, but not the customer.

Even with both a product and a customer, business still needs to make money by ensuring that the costs come in under the price that customers set in the marketplace. Although the pursuit of excessive profits leads to a whole host of exploitative conditions that give capitalism a bad reputation, we see profit as a relatively straightforward way that a market economy keeps score and ensures that value is being generated. As President Vaclav Havel of the Czech Republic once observed, "Though my heart may be left of center, I have always known that the only economic system that works is a market economy. This is the . . . only one that leads to prosperity."[1]

The inexorable demands for growth increasingly force companies to seek opportunities beyond their existing markets, potentially expanding into more unstable regions. Early successful entrants to these markets develop knowledge, assets, and relationships that will generate sustainable rewards. Indeed, the underdevelopment of frontline environments disproportionately rewards first movers. With annual economic activity estimated in the trillions of dollars, the frontlines represent the next lucrative frontier for business expansion.

Yes, there is a great deal of money to be made—but this healthy amount of self-interest doesn't preclude improving the lives of the poor. In fact, society increasingly calls upon companies to help solve the grand challenges of our day. Yet many executives resist these calls, seeing them in opposition to their duty to maximize shareholder wealth. Our experience shows this to be a false choice. Business can achieve both goals. It can turn a profit by operating in frontline environments, and in doing so, its investments can interrupt the endless cycle of poverty and conflict and clear the way for more economic opportunity.

When business starts to take hold in a community, it lays the foundation for many positive outcomes. Jobs provide not only income but also a sense of purpose and the dignity, identity, and outlet for talent that comes with a good day's work. Through work, a person can become independent and earn the means to look after their family and themselves. Children are less likely to go hungry and more likely to go to school. Houses get sturdy roofs. Building a successful business creates the possibility of the legacy of generational wealth. It also serves as a strong signal that a community is looking toward a more stable future. When a society is fearful of conflict, its members are less likely to make longer-term investments, like building a factory, purchasing equipment, or negotiating an extended contract. When there is too much risk, proprietors avoid doing even small things like painting walls or purchasing inventory in bulk. When the footprint of business investment becomes visible in communities, it encourages others to similarly plan for the future, creating a form of path dependence where business activity serves as further incentive for stability. This is the foundation upon which a community can thrive.

Let us be clear: we are not advocating for unbridled capitalism. We recognize that many people are skeptical that business can serve the common good and would rather have that role played by non-profit-seeking actors such as churches and community organizations. In 2023, the top eight richest billionaires own as much combined wealth as half of the human race.[2] We don't deny that alongside capitalism's economic engine often come the jagged edges of inequality and environmental destruction. However, the raw power of the private sector should not be underestimated. Incentivized, business simply gets work done. Particularly in places facing entrenched poverty and conflict, business is frequently the one part of society that provides incentives for people to invest in their enterprises, homes, and communities. Even more crucially, businesses and markets create the opportunity for repeated interactions among disparate members of society—the scaffolding upon which to build the relationships, social capital, and trust necessary for a resilient society.[3]

We are no more proponents of unchecked business than we are of unfettered charity or unilateral imposition of security through military action. Tackling the grand challenges of the twenty-first century such as poverty and conflict requires coordinated efforts from all sectors of society—no single sector can do it on its own. Social enterprises, humanitarian organizations, security forces, and local NGOs can all flourish alongside and in concert with business, using business principles and processes for the benefit of all.

Collaboration Is the Foundation of Business on the Frontlines

How exactly did two business school professors end up voluntarily embedded with the US Army Special Operations Forces? And how could our work end up changing the way companies conduct business around the world? It all started on the campus of the University of Notre Dame, where we were both professors in the Management Department at the Mendoza College of Business. No one would mistake us for a natural pair. When we first met, Emily misread Viva's reserve for rigidity, and Viva misdiagnosed Emily's informality for lack of seriousness. Viva carries a briefcase and has a soft spot for red suits and high heels. Emily prefers jeans and a backpack and was often mistaken for a student when accessing the faculty lounge. However, a mutual friend who could see past those differences insisted that we were kindred spirits. Over a lunch of pad see-ew at a four-table strip mall joint, we began to discover that our differences could prove to be the magic ingredient to enable us not only to rethink the role business could play in development and peace building but also to uncover the financial upside for companies that engaged in this work.

Disciplined and determined, Viva never met a challenge she would not embrace or a problem she could not solve with enough effort. Growing up as the child of World War II refugees from Lithuania instilled in her a deep commitment to serve others similarly impacted by war and suffering. In her teens, she ventured far from her close-knit Catholic immigrant family in Indiana to attend Yale and Oxford on a Rhodes Scholarship. For her doctoral research, she traveled alongside insurgents and guerillas in places like Tibet, Kurdistan, and South Sudan to understand why communities take up arms to fight wars of self-determination. She then joined McKinsey & Company, eventually being elected the youngest female partner in the Chicago office. In 2004, inspired by its mission to combine faith and reason in service of others, she joined the faculty of the University of Notre Dame and later the Board of Catholic Relief Services, where she found herself returning to many of the places she had studied for her dissertation. But now, with a decade of work in the private sector and several years as a business professor under her belt, she was keenly aware that the dynamism and energy of business was missing in efforts to serve those communities. In 2008, she founded the pioneering course, Business on the Frontlines (BOTFL), with the objective of harnessing business to reduce poverty and conflict in the world's toughest places.

Emily came to Notre Dame first as an undergraduate student. After a stint as a consultant with Anderson Consulting and earning her PhD at the University of Illinois, she returned to Notre Dame as a professor. She hoped to use her business scholarship, commitment to social justice, and organizational thinking to serve those in need. Fearless and independent, Emily's blended family made her adept at navigating large groups of people with disparate intentions and opinions. Comfortable in a world of ambiguity and unafraid to bear witness to pain, Emily wears her heart on her sleeve. People are drawn to her for both her clarity of thought and unflinching honesty. She often intentionally talks about taboos, including her own struggles with mental health and infertility, to create a more supportive and inclusive environment.

At lunch that day, Viva immediately recognized that Emily was the real deal. Emily had just returned from a trip to Lesotho to visit Touching Tiny Lives, a safe home for children suffering from HIV/AIDS. Emily's family had worked closely with the organization for years, and she was eager to leverage her business mindset to rethink how economic development could fight poverty. Despite their personality differences, their shared intensity, curiosity, and vision were apparent. One day, while walking across campus, Emily shared an insight on some problem that literally stopped Viva in her tracks. Unaccustomed to being presented with an alternative view that she had not already considered, Viva recognized what social psychologists have long demonstrated—novel ideas arise through the combination of vastly different perspectives. At that moment, Viva realized Emily might be the intellectual partner that she had not known she was looking for, and BOTFL found its second-in-command.

Building a friendship and partnership across both differences and shared commitment to service became a big part of what makes BOTFL so powerful. Once, when Lieutenant General Cleveland visited Notre Dame, Viva prepared her students to respect military protocol, insisting that they remain standing until the General sat down at the head of the table. Emily, in typical fashion, ran into the classroom like a tornado, made a beeline for the General, and gave him a huge hug. Viva shook her head at this breach of decorum, but at the same time, she recognized Emily's easygoing authenticity and ability to befriend everyone she encountered was part of what made their partnership work. Combined with Viva's diplomatic navigation of power and institutional authority, they make a powerful team. When working a problem in the field, Viva engages with CEOs, bishops, and Generals on the system changes needed while Emily gets the unvarnished scoop from the people on the ground.

prioritizes projects in places at risk of tipping back into conflict. This invariably leads to a focus on economic sectors that can employ large numbers of military-aged men, such as agriculture, mining, and infrastructure, so that we generate enough economic opportunities for the disenfranchised to have a stake in their own future and as an alternative to armed conflict. We work alongside action-oriented partners who coproduce innovative ideas with us and then spend years implementing them. The challenges our teams tackle are enormous, and no one initiative will change the world. In fact, we tell all our participants, "If we were tackling a problem that could be solved in six months with the concerted effort of even the best team of students, partners, advisors and professors, then it wouldn't be a problem worthy of our attention." Rather, through our ongoing commitment to frontline communities and organizations, we aim to transform their future trajectories for the better. And we persist, guided by the words of cultural anthropologist Margaret Mead: "Never doubt that a small group of committed citizens can change the world. Indeed, it is the only thing that ever has."[5]

In building this program, we have had a great deal of success and impact with both students and partners. Forbes named BOTFL one of the ten most innovative MBA courses in the United States. Donors provided a $35 million endowment to set it up as a permanent program at the University of Notre Dame. Because so many incoming MBA students say it was one of the top reasons they chose Notre Dame, the Mendoza College of Business redesigned its entire curriculum to make BOTFL its flagship program; once a selective offering to one, it is now accessible to all graduate business students. Eventually, we expanded the program further when Emily brought it with her to the University of Alberta, where she and her students have served partners and communities in Ethiopia, Ghana, Kyrgyzstan, and the Philippines. Other universities have begun to incorporate elements of BOTFL into their business school curricula.

To help us tackle our projects, we have been fortunate to convene teams of multinational corporations and world-class NGOs. General Electric, Newmont Mining, and Green Mountain Coffee Roasters have been among our many on-the-ground partners, along with leading humanitarian organizations like World Vision, Mercy Corps, and the Foundation for Amazon Sustainability. We have also partnered with a wide spectrum of religious and military organizations, from the Catholic Church to the US Army Special Operations Command. Leaders from companies like Intel, Amazon, Accenture, Procter & Gamble, and PricewaterhouseCoopers have been intimately involved as advisors on every project. Inspired by the belief in the power of business to do good in the world, professionals from these companies volunteer hours, days, and even months with us, working on specific problems, analyzing issues, traveling with us into the field, and lending their business expertise to market-making projects that we then test together on the ground. Through the process of deep collaboration with local partners, these business professionals bring novel insights back to their corporate headquarters—insights that have led to a number of follow-on cutting-edge initiatives.

Our experience in a wide range of cultures and societies shows that when we convene actors that might not normally collaborate—like Viva and Emily themselves—together we can imagine new and innovative approaches. Our aspiration is for BOTFL to become the forum for all organizations, no matter how diverse, to work together to build stable and prosperous societies. We prepare the table and offer a seat to anyone who would join us in good faith.

We are far from realizing this vision, however. We have been told many times by many people to stay in our lane. Our approach is not business as usual, and so it's difficult to counter generations of established routines. One long-standing NGO partner refused, at the last minute, to collaborate with a multinational corporation, despite pre-negotiated rules of engagement and demonstrated significant value for both parties. Another partner severed ties with our program because of our willingness to work with the US military. We understand the difficulties of forging unconventional partnerships. Humanitarian organizations face real risks when cooperating with the military. Many NGOs fear businesses will be too opportunistic. And businesses often question the relevance of NGOs and the military in their inherently economic calculations. However, when these groups share a common goal—to increase stability and economic opportunity—they can leverage their different perspectives, experiences, and skills to contribute to realizing this vision of a future of increased opportunity. Learning to collaborate across sectors is essential because none can accomplish these goals on its own. Our experience has shown time and again that when business teams up with public and private sectors, the results can improve lives and bottom lines.

As we built this unusual program, we have worn dirty boots as often as suits. In the course of fifteen years, we have collaborated on more than eighty growth-oriented projects across thirty-five countries. Together with our partners, we have created over thirty thousand jobs for those who would not otherwise have had work. The structure of the program provides us with an ongoing living laboratory to probe emerging ideas regarding development and conflict. You'll hear about some of these projects throughout this book—some successful, some not.[6] In all honesty, fully half of our projects have failed to have the impact on the ground that we aspired for them. But each failure provided an opportunity to reanalyze our process and mindset, learn from the experience, and make the changes necessary to increase the likelihood of success for subsequent projects. In this book, we share the lessons we have learned from this work in the frontlines so that leaders can successfully grow their businesses and make money in these challenging environments and, along the way, nudge societies toward a more prosperous and stable future.

Testing Out Our Approach in Senegal with the US Military

General Douglas MacArthur once said, "The soldier, above all others, prays for peace."[7] Unfortunately, most military interventions don't start until after the conflict has begun. To see whether they could get ahead of the violence, Lieutenant General Charles Cleveland was interested in working together to bring business and economics skills into his Special Forces' arsenal. A brilliant West Point graduate who led the largest unconventional war campaign since Vietnam, in northern Iraq in 2003, Cleveland is both the quintessential army General and a complete departure from the stereotype. He carries the authority of command naturally, regardless of whether he is wearing simple fatigues or his medal-adorned dress uniform. But his deep intellect and humility shines from under this formal authority. Cleveland and his team were deeply engaged in pioneering local partnerships so that his soldiers could gain legitimacy and influence in contests in which populations, rather than territory, were decisive. His hope was that if together we could determine the drivers of instability, then perhaps the US military could begin to engage in conflict prevention rather than conflict mitigation. Despite our rather rocky initial introduction at Fort Bragg, we were successful in creating a joint team of soldiers and business civilians to work toward those ends. The US Army Special Operations

Command (USASOC) decided to deploy our team to Senegal in West Africa.

Our team spent the first couple of weeks crisscrossing the country, visiting markets and mosques, fields and fishing boats, conference rooms and compounds. We spoke, mostly in French, to Senegalese farmers, traders, and fishermen. We visited religious leaders, government officials, aid workers, and business investors. It took only a short time for our team to find a productive rhythm, an appreciation of our complementary skills, and the basis of what would become lasting friendships.

One evening sitting in a cafe in Saint Louis, a colorful French colonial city on the border of Senegal and Mauritania, we compared notes as we watched the sun set over the Atlantic Ocean. The sea breeze did little to relieve our haggard crew from the heat that soaked our clothes in sweat. Flies circled our heads and drowned in our beers. That evening's conversation led to a breakthrough insight for the military: that the rapid expansion or widespread collapse of an entire economic sector in a territory could be a leading indicator of instability to come.[8] Moreover, we also realized that our team had stumbled upon not one but two such threats.

The possible collapse of the fishing industry in Senegal was the first indicator of potential future conflict. The military members of our team were concerned about overfishing by foreign open-water vessels and its negative impact on the fishing communities along the coast.[9] Many had been stationed in Djibouti and watched the rise of piracy after the collapse of the local fishing industry off the Somali coast.[10] However, in this case, we discovered that this potential threat could be averted, as the Senegalese fishers had already developed a low-tech but highly coordinated system of early warning and deterrence, using walkie-talkies and shotguns to push the foreign trawlers up to the Mauritanian coastline.

Our team became increasingly concerned about the recent discovery of the country's largest gold deposit, in Kedougou in eastern Senegal. It had generated a massive expansion of economic activity and quickly attracted thousands of illegal wildcat miners from other parts of Senegal and across the border from Guinea and Mali into this small region formerly populated by a few subsistence farmers. This type of mass migration put pressure on an already weak system of infrastructure, sanitation, and housing and brought with it crime, prostitution, and pollution. If that weren't disruptive enough, there was an undercurrent of unease among Senegalese religious leaders who had heard that enterprising Islamist extremists were heading to Kedougou to recruit from among the many unsuccessful and thus disappointed migrant miners who would be easy targets. It was clear to us that the discovery of gold was likely to not only create potential instability in Senegal but also exacerbate the crisis across the border in Mali, where profits from illegal mining could fuel the decade-long ongoing insurgency and terrorist activity. And unlike the fishing communities, no local initiative seemed to effectively neutralize the threat.

Our team of soldiers and civilians worked together to design a potential course of action in Kedougou, leveraging our respective expertise in security and business. This was a new experience for our soldiers, who were unaccustomed to focusing their attention on an area that was not yet in conflict, as they rarely get deployed until bullets start flying. Instead of their standard approach of focusing on regional security, we incorporated a number of social and economic initiatives into their deployment activities. Specifically, we focused on directing illegal miners toward legitimate employment, mainly in the expanding agricultural sector, and facilitated the presence of moderate religious leaders so that eastern Senegal wouldn't become a breeding ground for extremist religious terrorists. The emphasis on conflict prevention and the pragmatic interventions that contributed to stabilizing this region became the foundation for subsequent deployments and was incorporated into the curriculum for incoming Special Operations Forces soldiers.

Encouraged by this successful start, we moved on to a second project in Honduras and a number of other joint military-civilian initiatives until Lieutenant General Cleveland's retirement in 2015. Since then, other US Generals have requested our assistance to bolster their theater security plans with business outreach. The question is no longer whether the US military should take on an economic security role but how to do it. This approach, which Cleveland called operating in the Human Domain, is now an essential component of the USASOC mission.[11]

For us, the most salient indicator of success came from the soldiers themselves. In 2015, when Lieutenant General Cleveland presented Viva with the medal for US Special Operations Command's Outstanding Civilian Service, USSOCOM's highest civilian award, more than a dozen of the soldiers we had worked with traveled to South Bend to witness the presentation. That night, at Emily's house, filled with red wine and nostalgia, we asked the group what they had thought about us that first day at Fort Bragg. Joff Celleri, the Command Sergeant Major who had been most skeptical, leaned back in his chair and crossed his heavily tattooed arms over his broad chest.

"Honestly," he chuckled, "I thought 'what the fuck are you two little girls going to teach us about war?'"

"And now?" we inquired.

He smiled. "I can't stop thinking about how differently I would have spent $38 million dollars on the border of Afghanistan and Pakistan."

A Call for Business to Thrive and Improve Lives in the Frontlines

Our message—*that business can turn a profit and improve lives in some of the world's toughest places*—is directed both to business leaders and to leaders of other organizations, like NGOs and the military, who operate in frontline environments.

For business leaders, our approach should make good business sense. The unrelenting logic of growth demanded by shareholders inevitably requires businesses to seek out opportunities in increasingly unstable regions. We provide a replicable process that can help you understand and navigate both the challenges and opportunities inherent in such an expansion. Business leaders should find our perspective appealing because we argue that there need not be a trade-off between profit and impact. It is possible to earn money and simultaneously achieve nonfinancial goals such as corporate social responsibility, environmental conservation, and advancing social justice.

This message has already resonated with a wide variety of executives from diverse industries, including capital management, health care, technology, manufacturing, investment banking, and private equity. We also believe that this approach will appeal to business professionals who seek greater meaning through their work and hold a strong belief in the power of business to do good. We have seen evidence of this in the tens of millions of dollars and many hours of time many of them have donated to support our projects around the world. Our aspiration is to transform how current and future executives think about both the opportunity and the role of their organizations in the global landscape.

Our message is also directed to the leaders of the many public and nongovernmental organizations who have dedicated their lives to tackling the intractable challenges of poverty and conflict. Being open to partnering with business requires rethinking formerly entrenched patterns of interactions with members of the business community. However, we suggest that partnering with business can bring new resources, ideas, and pragmatism to solving the world's toughest problems.

In the first part of this book, we build the case for bringing business to the frontlines by describing both the opportunities for business and the benefits for communities that such collaborations may provide. In the second part of the book, we lay out the process that we use to access these opportunities. Throughout the book, we share both our greatest successes and our most humbling experiences, like diving under that folding table at Fort Bragg when the artillery shells exploded. We hope to illustrate what it looks like to take risks, to put yourself out there in novel ways, and to get your boots dirty by listening to and working with partners on the ground. There are incredible ideas and innovations waiting to be discovered in frontline environments. Those with the capacity to envision something new and the courage to do the hard work will play a role in changing our world for the better. Opportunity isn't always as far away as it looks.

PART I

The Opportunity

CHAPTER 1

The Juice Is Worth the Squeeze

It may not be business as usual, but by adopting our business model, using our process, and working with unusual partners, business can thrive while also improving lives in the frontlines.

I n 2010, as our dusty pickup truck crested the last hill before the town of Kasese in Western Uganda, our team grew more excited and anxious. Business on the Frontlines was in its infancy, and this was our first time returning to a community. It had been a year since our first project in this rural area, and we were all eager to find out what had happened since our departure. Western Uganda is a wild place, a large expanse with limited resources and overrun by marauding militias, those pouring over the border with the Democratic Republic of Congo and South Sudan or the country's own violent version—the Lord's Resistance Army. Our international humanitarian partner had asked us to support the efforts of several hundred subsistence farmers by finding buyers for their produce in the capital city of Kampala and beyond. We got to know many of these families by sitting in white plastic chairs in the shade of the mango trees and listening to their hopes for their kids—an education, a profession, a good marriage, or even small things like a new soccer ball.

Our day started at the crack of dawn in Kampala, with the sound of roosters and the smells of diesel, fried street food, and burning garbage. As guests at the archdiocesan compound, we eyed the luscious breakfast mangos, pineapples, and jackfruits, while quietly calculating how long politeness dictated that we remain at the table before we could hit the road. Traveling across 100 miles of Ugandan countryside could take five hours. But we were traveling much farther, 235 miles past Fort Portal to the westernmost side of the country. To navigate the poor roads, we would frequently need to pull wooden panels from the back of the four-by-four to drive over them, before replacing them into the back of the truck.

As we piled out of the truck in the town of Bundibugyo, which seemed much smaller than its booming population of 18,500, kids giggled, surrounding and welcoming us back. Some were even wearing the University of Notre Dame T-shirts we had brought as gifts the previous year, and a newborn was dressed in a festive Notre Dame sleeper. People congregated around our team and shared their meal. As expected, the village elder formally welcomed us back to his community. It was a raucous, joyous reunion.

During our previous visit, our team had diligently mapped the value chains of numerous fruits and vegetables—following all of the steps from planting the seeds to selling produce to consumers. Rather than interviewing government officials, international buyers, or others distant from the day-to-day realities of subsistence farmers, our team had organized its data gathering from the ground up, spending time with local traders, farmers, teachers, clergy, and other community leaders. Through this process, we also got to know the village elder's granddaughter, Dembe, whose name means "peace" in the local dialect.[1] A mother of five children, Dembe strapped her youngest daughter on her back with a colorful scarf while she worked. Besides running her household and cultivating a small plot of family land, Dembe also produced soap in her home to earn a bit of extra income.

Farmers like Dembe could earn much more for their crops if they were able to reach customers in the cities, including supermarkets and food processing companies, who paid ten times the price that she was getting from the middlemen who transported those goods to market. We conducted sensitivity analyses on all variables, such as input costs, quantity, quality, prices, and time, which demonstrated that, given the structure of the value chain, farmers could increase their profits if they stored their products securely and sold directly to urban consumers or processors in Kampala during the low season. We worked with the NGO staff and community leaders to organize cooperatives of up to 150 farmers to gain the economies of scale needed to capture these new market opportunities. The cooperatives purchased storage units and small trailers to hook onto motorcycles to transport and sell their crops directly to larger customers. We estimated that the profits would grow from 36,000 Ugandan shillings (UGX) (US$18) to 312,000 UGX (US$156) per farmer in the first three to five years. Although that may not seem like much money, it was enough to transform the lives of local families like Dembe's.

Upon our return, we saw many of the factors that we considered could indeed support a profitable enterprise. Over the past year, the rains had come and the harvest had been good. The new pesticides that the cooperative purchased were effective in controlling the crop-eating caterpillars, while the chunks of cassava left in the fields mollified the rats. Our NGO and community partners had delivered well-attended workshops around novel agricultural techniques to increase crop yields, and there had been an uptick in borrowing from their microfinance program to purchase quality seeds from reputable suppliers. The community members had selected respected members to lead the new cooperatives. It seemed that all the conditions were met for these new market arrangements to begin to bring benefits to the community.

However, there were no activities associated with the new farming cooperatives that we had helped launch the previous year. The recently built crop storage shed was gathering dust. Abandoned piles of maize were rotting on the sides of the roads. We expected to hear stories of trips to the Kampala markets to sell their produce, but there was no mention of it. We observed farmers feeding their surplus mangos and other fruits to their pigs. Instead of a new regional farmer's market filling one of the fields in town, the space hosted an impromptu game of soccer between local kids and our team.

As the sun set over the fields, our disheartened team wandered over to a patch of grass under the mango trees where we joined Dembe and other young mothers watching their toddlers play. Viva confessed that she missed her own young daughter, Ava. In the quiet twilight, Dembe revealed the real reason why our ideas had not been successful. Not long after the first harvest was transported to Kampala, a group of men with guns invaded a village meeting and kidnapped five of the cooperative leaders. They were held for hours until they agreed to abandon the new market ventures. The kidnappers were the middlemen. The new arrangements, particularly the direct sales contracts between the recently launched cooperatives and Kampala customers, threatened both their profits and their regional position. Their response was to use guns to take back their lost power. The farmers had no recourse. They could not call the police; they were located far away, and even if they had been closer, chances are they were on the take from the middlemen.[2] In these faraway places, communities often must fend for themselves.

As President Dwight D. Eisenhower once pointed out, "Plowing looks mighty easy when your plow is a pencil and you're a thousand miles from the corn field."[3] In our attempt to create sustainable markets that would enhance the household incomes of our subsistence farmers, we had missed one incredibly important element: our competition.

As is often the case with our work in frontline environments, we found ourselves having to start over at the beginning, rethinking our assumptions and reworking the problem. How could we understand the competition? Here, being "Mzungu" was an asset. Middlemen, assuming our ignorance of the landscape, were surprisingly willing to meet with us, and most importantly, they were willing to leave their guns behind. We asked them far-ranging questions, such as, "Tell us about your family. . . . Tell us about your dreams." And we then spent hours listening until things started to make more sense.

We learned that most of these middlemen had strong family connections to the surrounding villages. Some identified themselves as brothers, cousins, sons, fathers, or uncles.[4] They had not always been men with guns, and many shared aspirations for a more reputable future, including having a family, building their own house, or starting a business. Many yearned for a sense of belonging to their communities as legitimate members, not as outlaws. Many also wished to be respected enough to gain permission to marry someone's daughter.

With this new information, we asked ourselves how many middlemen would need to shift their allegiance to protect the cooperatives for the program to succeed? We have learned, in Kasese and in other places we have worked, that the answer is surprisingly low. We needed about a quarter of the existing middlemen, just 25 percent, to throw their weight behind new market arrangements for the new way of doing business to survive. In this case, the community members themselves decided that it was worth it to work with some of the middlemen and took the lead in identifying and approaching the ones who they thought they could bring into the fold. The community offered them a better deal, which included ownership in the cooperatives. These new recruits gave the cooperatives enough protection to begin shifting their sales away from the middlemen to other mainly urban customers. The remaining armed middlemen disappeared, shifting their focus to weaker and less organized communities. Years later, when an international education NGO decided to build a primary school in Bundibugyo, parents in the cooperative had the funds to pay for books, supplies, and uniforms needed to send their kids to the new school.

Welcome to the Frontlines

Frontline environments are isolated, lawless areas stuck in a recursive cycle of poverty and violence. They teeter on the razor's edge between stability and chaos—emerging from war or poised to tip back into conflict. They sit at a critical juncture where every decision, event, or investment could mean the difference between encouraging the society toward opportunity or sending it into conflict. These places present many challenges for business, but they are also ripe with undeveloped potential.

Frontline environments do not follow national borders and can be found hiding inside countries with wealthy or peaceful areas. As such, they are not always easy to identify. Because of their geographic isolation, they are often only nominally part of a country's infrastructure—national governments do not extend basic security and rule of law to a frontline territory, nor do they administer services that address the basic needs of the citizens who live there. For example, walking through the Garden City Mall in Kampala, Uganda's capital, you would be hard pressed to recognize that you were in a country classified as low income by the World Bank. A luxury shopping center with high-end shoe shops, clothiers, and restaurants, it feels a world away from Kasese, where the long shadows of poverty and war still touch everyday life.[5]

In the frontlines, security is frequently left to local militias or cartels who recruit military-aged men with few opportunities for alternative livelihoods. These criminal organizations often participate in predatory economic activities that accumulate more profits than traditional market mechanisms would normally permit. These activities may look like business, but if you need a gun to enforce a contract, then it is not business. The lawlessness, isolation, and lack of infrastructure serve as a barrier for other actors in society to enter and rebalance the situation. And as this pattern of activity gets entrenched, it creates a recursive cycle of poverty and conflict that is difficult to break. Oxford economist Paul Collier's work has demonstrated that nearly half of the poorest countries who emerge from war will tip back into conflict within the next decade.[6]

Despite their instability, the frontlines are full of possibilities. Largely overlooked in the past wave of globalization, the frontlines reflect the next great frontier of global business. Their dynamism and untapped potential combined with populations with a strong aspiration to a better life can drive change in these societies. The business opportunities we uncovered in Western Uganda are representative of broader prospects in frontline environments. Business is everywhere—even the most remote rural village is teeming with economic activity. And businesses are always expanding, forever looking for new undeveloped markets. Business can thrive there while simultaneously laying a foundation that helps tip these societies toward the path to greater stability, opportunity, and dignity.

The remainder of this chapter outlines the location and magnitude of economic activity in the frontlines and its drivers of ongoing growth. Yet accessing the full transformative potential of these burgeoning economic opportunities will require a departure from business as usual. And thus, we will also outline strategic options for businesses to access this potential in the frontlines.

In Uganda, business as usual might look like executives from a major international food processor arriving in Kampala to diversify their company's sources of supply. They would follow the usual advice contained in international business textbooks, starting with building local relationships. They might begin with the various government-supported export boards or local food processors in the capital city that they identified online. They may even exit their air-conditioned hotel conference room to visit the big open-air Owino Market, perhaps ordering a delicious "Rolex," an omelet wrapped in an Indian chapati. However, odds are that their local Ugandan business associates would help them broker a supply contract with the middlemen from Kasese instead of the newly launched local cooperatives. Of course, both parties would be thrilled with the deal. The foreign executives would have secured a local supplier, and the middlemen would receive a windfall in the form of the major export contract. Nevertheless, it is likely that the executives would not recognize the fragility of this arrangement. The cooperative farmers would have no incentive to grow reliably high-quality fruits and vegetables, as the middlemen always pay the same low prices (which they impose by monopoly and fear) regardless of the quality of the produce. And thus, inadvertently, business as usual would perpetuate the exploitative economic relationships that created the conditions for instability in the first place.

Another version of business as usual would be an international corporation trying to reduce the risks of market expansion by controlling as much of the value chain as possible—from raw material inputs through transportation and sales. Doing so requires heavy upfront capital investment to develop new infrastructure. The approach has been successful in places like India and China, whose large domestic markets, single regulatory framework, and stable governance enable the amortization of any expansion across a large enough business volume to reduce investment uncertainty. However, in smaller, fragmented, insecure, and complex frontline environments, this traditional international expansion strategy will likely not yield attractive returns on investment.

Instead, we present a different way that business can successfully operate in the frontlines. First, we demonstrate that the frontlines represent the next wave of globalization, that there is sufficient market size, growth potential, and limited competition to attract investment. Next, we identify the entry point in which companies, both foreign and domestic, can take advantage of high-growth opportunities based on a set of underdeveloped and underutilized resources. Further, we outline how organizations can position themselves at strategic points in the value chain, using a lean and flexible business model, and we recommend a partnership approach to complement their targeted investment. And finally, we describe the novel skills and capabilities that businesses must develop to execute this approach. Throughout this book, we illustrate how we have developed this approach over fifteen years of experience working on eighty projects in more than thirty-five frontline environments.

The Frontlines Represent $20 Trillion in Economic Opportunity

At the beginning of the twenty-first century, rapid technological innovations and geopolitical changes brought with them new economic opportunities on a global scale. The publication of both Thomas Friedman's *The World Is Flat* and C. K. Prahalad's *Fortune at the Bottom of the Pyramid* documented the ways that businesses captured these opportunities in a race toward globalization. Friedman argued that as communication costs essentially approach zero through the convergence of the personal computer with fiber optic cable and workflow software, entire business models would be disentangled, allowing the labor components to be outsourced to low-cost economies such as India and China.[7] Prahalad described how business could tap into immense market potential and innovative energy by engaging with the poorest four billion people on the planet (who, at that time, earned less than two dollars per day).[8]

Although estimates vary widely, the sums invested in emerging markets from 2000 to 2020 surpassed trillions of dollars.[9] Most of this expansion focused on large markets such as China, India, and Brazil—locations that have a single legal framework and reasonable governance—or into large urban centers in more fragile countries, like Kampala, Uganda, or Bogota, Colombia. In these cities, governments provided a measure of stability by recognizing property rights, enforcing contracts, and upholding the rule of law, and they welcomed businesses that could grow their economies. During this first wave of globalization, the most accessible developing markets benefited from the lion's share of investment. However, many senior executives now fear their investments in these locations will begin to yield diminishing marginal returns.[10] The logic of growth so central to business will require expansion into less developed territories, including those with weaker governance and less institutional infrastructure. This will usher in a new wave of globalization focused on the frontlines.

However, the strategies that drove success during the first round of international expansion will not be sufficient or appropriate in the frontlines. It is not just that the rules of the game are different—successfully operating in environments characterized by poverty and violence is fundamentally a different game. Profit is still the way to keep score, but the tools, processes, and resources required to succeed are different. One of the aims of this book is to help businesses understand this unfamiliar environment and what is required for success. Through our research and experiences, we have seen how it is possible to generate real economic returns in the frontlines. When businesses follow our approach, they can reduce risks, cut costs, and increase profits, all while interrupting the endless cycle of poverty and conflict and clearing the way for more economic opportunities.

To make the case that businesses should expand into frontline environments, we first need to understand the location and magnitude of economic activity in those areas. We begin with the universally used classification from the World Bank that sorts countries according to their level of development: low, lower-middle, upper-middle, and upper income. Prahalad included countries that fell into low- and lower-middle-income categories to denote "Bottom of the Pyramid" markets, while Collier argued that only a subset of low-income countries made up the population of interest in his "Bottom Billion."

Like Collier, we suggest that the World Bank's classification must be modified, as it both underestimates the economic activity in frontline environments and mischaracterizes the whereabouts of those opportunities.

The World Bank classification system is problematic for our purposes, as it treats each country as a coherent unit. However, we argue that frontline environments cannot be defined according to national borders owing to the vast income inequalities between the urban elites and the rural population. This is true in both the poorest countries (low and lower-middle income) and in emerging economies (upper-middle income) where cities like Jakarta, Indonesia, and Nairobi, Kenya, already teeming with business investment, are not reflective of the reality of the whole country. Rural areas, even those located in upper-middle-income countries such as South Africa and Guatemala, are much more difficult to penetrate but represent overlooked and underdeveloped opportunities. Thus, we suggest that any calculation of frontline markets should exclude urban populations in lower- and lower-middle-income countries and include rural populations in upper-middle-income countries.[11] We also recognize that some lower- and middle-income environments are simply not amenable to sustainable business investment at this time. As such, we exclude active war zones, such as Syria and Ukraine, as the level of unpredictability means that risks far outweigh any opportunities. We also exclude Russia and North Korea because investment by most countries is prohibited by international sanctions.[12] Finally, we excluded China and India as they were the main focus of the first wave of globalization and are largely saturated by large amounts of earlier international expansion.

To calculate the magnitude of economic activity within frontline environments, it is necessary to move beyond traditional country measures of economic output, like gross domestic product (GDP). In addition to the geographical limitations, these measures are not sufficient for two reasons. First, because many commodities like food are cheaper in low-income and lower-middle-income countries, their residents can buy more of them, thereby extending their purchasing power and living standards. As a result, the absolute value of any opportunity is likely to be underestimated. We correct this by standardizing these differences across countries using what economists term "purchasing power parity." This approach compares the price of a given basket of goods and services across different locations and translates those costs into a comparable currency. It allows us to more accurately reflect the amount of economic activity in the region.

Second, these measures underestimate economic activity because they include only formal activities, excluding the informal economy from a country's tax base and GDP. In the frontlines, informal work is likely to be at least as important, if not more so, in people's daily lives than the formal economy. Most rural farmers and tradespersons do not concern themselves with legal incorporation or taxes. We encountered an example of this while working in Ethiopia on a project to construct a well-engineered, massive dam to increase access to water and sanitation in a large, remote, dry region of the country. Accustomed to working with formal corporate entities in Addis Ababa, our partner was frustrated by the lack of receipts for raw materials for their accounting processes. When we arrived at the construction site, we immediately saw why this was the case. Local villagers delivered the rocks for concrete in wheelbarrows and were paid by weight in cash. These "suppliers" weren't formal organizations. They didn't have a tax ID number, nor could they provide the required receipts. They operated outside of the formal economy. In fact, based on household surveys, electricity

damage, the larger point remains that making specific adjustments to the land at scale can have powerful economic impact.

In addition to agriculture, the natural resources sector is severely underinvested, as a majority of this mineral wealth remains undiscovered. The extractive value of each square kilometer of land in developed countries averages $125,000. The same area in Africa is estimated at only $25,000.[17] Geological factors cannot account for this discrepancy. Rather, it reflects the sheer level of underdevelopment of these resources.[18] Whether and how frontline societies that own these minerals decide to permit their extraction and then manage their bounty is up to their citizens, as histories with natural resource extraction have often resulted in high levels of corruption and increased economic inequality. However, the point remains that prospecting investments in these areas are likely to yield significant discoveries that, managed ethically and sustainably, can also yield significant financial upside. Given the bounty on which many frontline environments sit, investment in natural resource development is likely one of the first steps toward economic prosperity in these regions.

Investment in agriculture, mining, and infrastructure is also likely to provide an additional and simultaneous benefit to frontline societies: security. These economic sectors require a large number of employees and are traditionally male oriented. This is particularly valuable in societies under threat of conflict, as a lack of economic opportunity is often one of drivers for young men to take up arms by joining insurgencies, militias, or criminal organizations. These particular economic sectors provide the benefit of large-scale employment to military-aged men, thereby generating sufficient livelihoods for the disenfranchised to have a stake in their own future. Given the benefits of agriculture and natural resources in frontline environments, many of the examples that we use in this book will come from these sectors.

A second driver of growth, and one that is particularly relevant in the frontlines, is labor. Growth here requires either an untapped source of labor or the ability to improve the average productivity of workers. Both are the case in the frontlines. These societies have expanding workforces, with young and growing populations. More young people means that the economy is able to produce more work. In addition, frontline economies are often characterized by high levels of unemployment and underemployment. This signals that the labor market can absorb more workers without drastically driving up wages, which would make it more costly for companies to operate there. On average, frontline environments have lower levels of education than more urban or developed regions. As a result, modest investments in education and training can improve the productivity levels of the existing workforce. This creates a self-perpetuating cycle: when education levels improve, so do health outcomes, enabling people to contribute more to the economy.[19]

Similarly, weak frontline infrastructure can be bolstered with modest improvements in technology. Investment-constrained frontline markets can translate even small amounts of targeted capital into disproportionate returns. Examples could be as simple as a greenhouse to grow seedlings, which would have higher yields than basic seeds when replanted in the fields. It could also include the purchase and use of pesticides and fertilizer. Alternatively, even basic food processing equipment such as drying racks for fruits and vegetables can increase the value and longevity of agricultural produce. Investments in basic transportation such as motor bikes and trailers to carry these products to urban markets where customers pay higher prices also earn an attractive payback.

In the frontlines, first movers reap the rewards. We suggest that early entrants to frontline markets should target underutilized land, labor, and capital to generate potential disproportionate returns.[20] Beginning with opportunities that take advantage of underdeveloped natural resources and deploying technology and capital to improve productivity can create a self-reinforcing cycle that drives further economic development. These early investments have a snowball effect on the adjacent rural economy, thereby increasing demand for follow-on economic sectors such as consumer products, banking services, and telecommunications. As disposable incomes rise, people can afford nonessential items, and consumption increases. This fuels further growth in the consumer goods, retail, and service sectors. These developments become the foundation for the economic growth trajectory as communities work over many years to catch up and ultimately converge with wealthier societies.

Own the Essential Activities and Partner the Rest

Effectively conducting business in the frontlines requires being particularly selective about which parts of the industry value chain to invest in and which parts to outsource to strategic partners. The value chain consists of all the activities associated with creating a product or service in a given sector, from raw materials all the way to end customers. Many traditional approaches to expansion into emerging markets manage the inherent uncertainty and instability in these geographies by attempting to control all aspects of the value chain. However, in frontline environments, this is nearly impossible and certainly prohibitively expensive. Our approach eschews purchasing land, establishing plantations, hiring a large, dedicated workforce, providing financing, and controlling distribution, which would require a significant upfront investment that would take too long to earn a reasonable payback.

Rather, we emphasize owning only those steps in the value chain where you have a distinct competitive advantage based on unique assets or capabilities and then cultivating relationships with a wide variety of local (and nontraditional) partners to conduct all the other activities in the value chain.

For example, a food processor or supermarket chain looking to work in a frontline environment should focus on those elements of the value chain where it holds a competitive advantage: in most cases, access to customers in large markets and quality control. To make the operations across the entire value chain work, the company would then need to partner with small local farmers to supply produce, local NGOs to provide training to improve quality and yields, and banks and microfinance institutions to provide access to credit for modest purchases of fertilizer or pesticides. Although there are additional operating expenses associated with managing the complexity of these untraditional partnerships across the value chain, these operating costs are more than offset by the significant reduction in upfront investment. Such a capital-light expansion approach not only means higher returns on investment but also spurs experimentation across smaller markets and enables flexibility and resilience.

This light footprint can be achieved only by partnering directly with the variety of actors that already operate in the frontlines. And they are often very different from the partners business traditionally works with. For example, businesses expanding internationally are accustomed to working with national governments. Even when embedded in countries with established governments, frontline environments rarely benefit from the more effective governance experienced in the large cities. What governance exists can often be inept, corrupt, or controlled by powerful illegal actors, leaving communities to fend for themselves. This creates a void that is filled by humanitarian organizations and domestic and international military forces.

Our project in Western Uganda illustrates this wide range of players beginning with the largely absent national government. The local administration was appointed by Kampala and, given its ineffectiveness, lacked popular support. Most services that would normally be delivered by the government were provided by NGOs, including clean water, sanitation, health care, and education. Ideally, NGOs would serve only as temporary intermediaries to fill the void of these essential services until such time as the government could take over. However, in reality, our partner was one of more than two thousand NGOs registered in the country, many of whom had been serving in Uganda for decades.[21]

This part of Uganda was disputed territory where the government could not extend basic security and rule of law. The remnants of rebel forces of the Lord's Resistance Army (which the US government has designated a terrorist organization) have drawn the presence of soldiers, both from the Uganda People's Defense Force and US Army Special Operations Forces deployed in the region since 2009.[22] All these groups in Western Uganda have dabbled in economic activities, but none has succeeded in jump-starting economic growth. In many contested frontline areas, some groups step into the power vacuum by winning the hearts and minds of the people living there, providing basic services and enough predictability that people can continue to live their lives. More often, however, they exert control through coercion, force, and fear.

Operating in the frontlines requires business to develop new skills to navigate among these different actors. Success depends on leveraging the strengths of some and negotiating a basic understanding with others. Operating in this way also requires that businesses become deeply embedded in local communities—so much so that the community begins to perceive the success of the business as akin to their own. This integration cannot be achieved by a single interaction but rather requires a web on ongoing relationships based on mutual benefit. To illustrate, by purchasing their supplies locally, businesses can build up local commerce. Overall, it will require finding ways to introduce business principles and processes to bring potential partners together to achieve their common objectives.

Early Success in the Frontlines

Some businesses that we have worked with have already achieved success using these principles. Founded in 1978 in Quezon City, Jollibee is a Filipino fast-food chain that operates 1,500 restaurants in Southeast Asia and is rapidly popping up in Western cities. We worked with them, in conjunction with Catholic Relief Services, an international humanitarian organization, to overcome an acute shortage in onions, an essential condiment in Filipino hamburgers. To achieve this, Jollibee brought together a multitude of actors to develop a rural entrepreneurship program to connect with, train, and invest in small farmers on the war-torn island of Mindanao to access the Jollibee supply chain. The US Department of Agriculture contributed training manuals to improve farming techniques. Alalay sa Kaunlaran, a local microfinance institution, provided access to small loans to upgrade farming equipment. This collaboration organized more than two thousand farmers into fifteen cooperatives to gain the scale needed to interact with Jollibee. During the first couple of harvests, the farmers' onions failed to meet the quality requirements dictated by Jollibee. It took three to five years for most of them to get it right. But since that time, the effort has paid off. They have even expanded to other crops, including tomatoes, bell peppers, lemons, and chilis. These local farmers now supply 25 percent of the vegetables used in Jollibee's Filipino restaurants.[23]

We also worked with Comfandi, the Colombian social service organization that runs the largest supermarket chain in the country. Comfandi has built a similar network of partners to support its purchases of local produce to sell in its supermarkets.[24] Beginning in 2017, and starting with eight hundred marginalized Indigenous and Afro-Colombian farmers, the program has continued to expand, mainly through organizing more farmers into selling associations and providing them access to banking services. This program has guaranteed Comfandi's vegetable supply while also improving the livelihoods of the rural poor.

In the case of Jollibee and Comfandi, working with local small-scale producers provides both businesses with significant benefits. Although these arrangements often guarantee prices to the small farmers, such guarantees also smooth out purchases and sales during times of price volatility for both buyer and supplier. The additional value in developing relationships with small suppliers is that in times of crisis—a drought, a hurricane, a global pandemic—supplies are frequently constrained. Relationships are likely to matter for farmers when faced with choices about which customers to prioritize. When a large business works with a small supplier, they are often their most important customer and will be first in line to gain supply while their competitors, who go through market intermediaries, will have to wait their turn.

Any corporation, regardless of the location of their headquarters, can team up with public and nonprofit sectors to reduce risks, cut costs, and increase profits in frontline markets. To work with these organizations, business requires openness to different interests and perspectives and a degree of flexibility in its own processes. However, the opportunity to make money while contributing to resilient societies and providing individuals with the dignity of a good day's work become compelling motivations to experiment along these dimensions.

The Time Is Now for Business on the Frontlines

Business leaders are increasingly being called upon to contribute innovative solutions to the urgent grand challenges facing humanity. However, these calls are often perceived as butting up against the hard logic of economics, which prioritizes shareholder wealth maximization. Our experience shows this to be a false dichotomy. Business can achieve both goals—it can turn a profit by operating in frontline environments, and in doing so, it can nudge societies toward a more prosperous and stable future. Where our approach has succeeded, we have changed thinking and improved lives. Working with our partners around the world, our projects have created more than thirty thousand jobs. We celebrate each one of those jobs, as it represents an opportunity for a family to have a better life.

But we admit the work isn't easy. Going against the conventional wisdom and divesting control of parts of the value chain is counterintuitive. Cross-sector partnerships with the plurality of actors in frontline environments can take time to develop and maintain. But business brings a distinct skill set, pragmatism, and perspective and, thus, is key to fundamentally transforming societies. It creates value for customers based on a series of voluntary market transactions that also provide opportunities for peaceful interaction between opposing parties. Over time, those repeated interactions can provide the frame upon which deeper relationships, social capital, and trust can develop. Business is self-sustaining and growth oriented based on the discipline of the market and does not require continued bolstering from donors. In the frontlines, business changes the dynamic by providing alternatives for people to engage in dignified work. However, business cannot do it alone. Businesses must learn to collaborate and leverage the knowledge and capabilities of the other actors in the space. Good relationships with local communities, NGOs, and military forces can provide business with the security knowledge to operate more safely. Business must become adept at navigating the gray moral and operational challenges of working in places where power is often held by those outside the government. However, as we learned with the armed middlemen in Kasese, they are human beings who are often victims of their circumstances and who may be amenable to an alternate way of life. The opportunity to participate in society and the dignity of a good day's work are compelling motivations drawing even those on the fringe of society into legitimate work.

And because this work is tough, we look to the stories of the individuals whose lives are transformed as a source of inspiration: people like Heliadora, a widow of the Colombian civil war, who supported her three children by growing coca—the main ingredient for cocaine. During our long conversations on her tiny one-hectare plot of land, where pale green coca plants poked out of the darker green of the jungle's foliage, we learned about her hopes for her family—a steady income, education for her kids, a safe home. Yet from the Colombian government's perspective, Heliadora was running an illegal enterprise. A military option—like simply increasing Colombian army patrols to manually remove her coca crops and keep the narco-traffickers off her land—wasn't feasible in such a remote and inaccessible part of the country. Nor would a charitable option help here: NGO assistance to start growing new crops would not accommodate her lost income or feed her kids until harvest.

Rather, from our diagnosis, Heliadora faced a business problem. She needed bridge capital to help her survive the initial 30 percent financial penalty from exiting coca cultivation to grow legal crops such as pumpkins and lemons. She also needed guaranteed customers and a low-cost way to transport her goods to market. With the assistance of Colombia's leading peace-building NGO, we contributed business principles and hard-nosed pragmatism into the mix. Together, we developed a pathway to a new life. And thus, Heliadora and her fellow *cocaleras* (coca-growing farmers) took small initial steps and began learning to grow and sell legal crops.

Rural Colombia represents a classic frontline environment: poor, isolated, with the constant threat of violence, in this case from drug cartels. All of us—Heliadora, her neighbors, NGO staff, and our team—understood the facts on the ground. If only one or two families tried to exit coca, the narco-traffickers would send their thugs to the farms to issue threats to maintain their supply of coca. A few campesinos could not oppose the drug lords, but an entire community of farmers in a remote valley might just stand a shot at escaping their intimidation. And thus, for Heliadora and her neighbors to have a chance at a life outside the shadows, they organized a unified front of campesinos, even collaborating with those in society who had earlier ostracized them for cultivating coca. They would all exit at the same time to force the criminals to conduct their own calculations and perhaps decide it was easier to seek coca leaf supply elsewhere. With the NGO staff accompanying them each step of the way, these brave women quietly launched a cooperative to sell their legal produce. Lacking sufficient sales outlets for their goods, the women also organized regional campesino markets to bring together both customers and producers.

By day, Heliodora was sowing and tilling her small farm by hand. By night, with only the light of one small lamp in her modest one-room home, Heliodora studied alongside her three children. She was educating herself on basic accounting principles so that she could take over administration of the cooperative. We asked Heliodora why she was working so hard and taking such risks to make this cooperative business a success. She confided that being from a coca-growing family would limit the social mobility of her children. She hoped that if she could move into more respectable employment, then "quizás entonces mi hija podrá casarse con un buen chico" (maybe then my daughter can marry a nice boy). Heliadora paid back the modest loan from the NGO in under two years. Now with every harvest and successful sale, she is gradually building back up to her previous income level and enjoying more economic freedom. Today she feels safer and happier, and, more importantly, her three children are enrolled in school.

Heliadora's story reminds us not only of the incredible efforts needed to transform frontline environments, but also of the ultimate advantages for both businesses and those working hard to make them successful. As Lieutenant General Charlie Cleveland more colorfully puts it, the juice is worth the squeeze.

We have established the frontlines, with its nearly $20 trillion in annual economic activity, as an attractive expansion opportunity for business. But how can businesses gain access to these uncertain and unstable environments? How can they mitigate the security risk to their people and property? The next chapter explores different entry strategies for business to thrive in the frontlines.

CHAPTER 2

Security Is Not a Fixed Cost

Policies that embed businesses into frontline communities can re-
duce security costs, creating attractive opportunities for investors as
well as increasing stability for locals.

O n our way to the corporate headquarters of General Electric (GE),
we drove through the affluent suburban landscape of Fairfield,
Connecticut, passing grand houses with perfectly manicured lawns.
Officially, we were going to meet with some of the company's top executives to interview them about their strategic decision-making processes. But because GE operated in so many emerging markets around
the world, we were also hoping to recruit the company as a multinational corporate partner for Business on the Frontlines.

Getting out of the car, we felt a jolt of cognitive dissonance as we
inhaled a breath of freshly mowed grass. GE's corporate headquarters
were a world away from the dusty areas where we regularly traveled
and worked—places where homes often had dirt floors and thatched

roofs, kids ran around without shoes, and the regular sight of guns kept us vigilant. There, we might smell a freshly slaughtered chicken frying not far from where its blood pooled on the soil. Here, the smell was sweet, and the only blood we could imagine seeing would be from a paper cut. Bridging this gap between immaculate corporate offices and gritty frontline worlds was our mission, so we went inside to see what we could learn.

We spent most of our day with Frank Taylor, a retired Air Force General and former undersecretary of homeland security for intelligence and analysis under President Barack Obama, who served as GE's executive vice president for security. He held two degrees from the University of Notre Dame and was one of the first African American airmen to be promoted to the rank of Brigadier General. We observed that no one at GE called him Frank, or even Mr. Taylor. It was always "General." Despite his towering and commanding presence, he was welcoming. Rather than sending an assistant, as so many executives would, Taylor came to the lobby and greeted us himself.

In 2011, GE ranked eighth in the Fortune 500, just behind Apple and General Motors (and ahead of AT&T and Ford). Its global footprint was massive, with operations across roughly 130 countries, and its infrastructure work was vital to keeping many of those economies running. In addition to manufacturing airplane engines and medical diagnostic equipment, GE also produced huge electrical turbines for power plants. A critical ingredient to economic development, a reliable and consistent power supply is frequently difficult to secure in the frontlines. We hoped that developing a closer relationship with GE would give us insights into this persistent challenge.

When we asked about his most difficult business challenge during his time at GE, Taylor didn't hesitate. "The Arab Spring," he said. He showed us a picture of the location of GE's Cairo headquarters over-looking Tahrir Square. For a month in 2011, the square was jammed with an estimated three hundred thousand protesters. The air was electric with rage and the potential for violence. Although GE had many locations in the Middle East where unrest exploded, in Egypt they literally had a front row seat. A once-in-a-generation international populist uprising like the Arab Spring created an unprecedented crisis. But Taylor told us that GE's security procedures—meticulously developed and refined from operating in other unstable places that fell short of outright revolution, like the Philippines and Colombia—were well organized and precisely planned to reduce vulnerability.

In the event of a crisis, his first priority is to take care of GE's staff. He and his team must determine the best way to evacuate expats quickly and identify the locations where local staff should shelter in place. The next priority is infrastructure. This includes anticipating the costs of quickly shuttering factory and distribution operations, as well as preparing to float loans to suppliers to protect the future supply chain and managing inventory levels in case of protracted disruptions to operations. "Then and only then, can the country manager start figuring out if the local GE business can still make money," he added.

We were struck by the matter-of-fact way he described operating under such conditions of chaos. We remembered the times we had found ourselves in the middle of a crisis. Evacuating from Nairobi into the countryside when election violence erupted. Being stranded during a tsunami in the Philippines. We imagined panicked calls from stranded expats and local employees desperately trying to contact their families. How does he ensure that the process doesn't break down?

"We practice."

"What do you mean practice?" we asked. "Like a rehearsal?"

"Exactly."

"But how do you know what to practice for? How do you anticipate what can go wrong?"

"Let me show you."

Taylor led us through a door that looked like an emergency exit and down a flight of concrete stairs to the basement. We entered a darkly lit room the size of a basketball court. "This is our Global Watch Center," Taylor said. Analysts sat in rows, monitoring political, civic, and economic events like strikes or natural disasters in real time on their screens. Across one wall was a giant interactive global map, a Jumbotron-like amalgamation of screens that must have been fifteen feet high and fifty feet long. It was here that Taylor and his security team were able to keep track of the movements of GE's top one thousand managers when they work abroad so that they could respond to any potential threats to their personnel before they got out of hand. They monitor every place on the globe where GE operates, each country on the screen lit up with lights marking the exact location of their offices, factories, and distribution centers. The room buzzed with intensity. It felt like a scene out of a movie. "I cannot sit in Fairfield and direct daily security operations. We have to empower our local and regional managers to translate, consistently and regularly, GE security procedures into their daily responsibilities, developing security contingencies as needed." And thus, it was from the Global Watch Center that Taylor and his team orchestrated frequent fire drills, where multiple times a year each office gets surprised by a simulated level 1, 2, or 3 disaster and practices their response.

GE's approach to security was thorough and appealing. The idea that a company would dedicate so much time and so many resources to maintaining such high standards of safety and security for its people and assets was inspiring. We thought to ourselves that if we were ever to work in the Democratic Republic of the Congo, which has been embroiled in armed conflict for the past three decades, we would want GE as a partner.

But GE's approach is also expensive. Prohibitively expensive for all but the largest and most profitable multinational corporations. It requires a level of technical sophistication that few are able to attain. Plus, there are not that many retired former Generals willing to work as hard as Taylor postretirement to whip a company's security processes into shape.

From our perspective, GE's approach to security was the gold standard, but we wondered whether other companies could even get close. If such a high level of investment is needed, we didn't think there would be a long line of companies rushing to expand into frontline environments. Little did we know, we were about to meet someone with a radically different but equally effective approach to security.

Creating Security in Ghana Through Embedding Operations in Frontline Communities

Most of us never give a thought to where the precious metals in our jewelry and electronics come from. Quietly, without making headlines, one Fortune 500 company dominates this lucrative mining industry: Newmont Mining. The leading mining company in the United States and the world's top gold miner, Newmont was founded in Montana in 1916 and grew rapidly, exploring and mining for gold, silver, copper, lead, zinc, lithium, uranium, coal, and nickel. Expanding beyond the American West, Newmont developed enormous mines as far afield as Yanacocha, Peru, and Batu Hijau, Indonesia. By the early 2000s, it employed more than forty thousand people in operations that stretched across five continents.

Large-scale mineral extraction is frequently the first industrialized activity that local residents in poor, remote areas ever experience. Although some players in the mining industry are notorious for disregarding both safety and the environment, Newmont had a long track record of commitment to miner safety, environmental protection, and zero tolerance for corruption. For these reasons, and because of its work in unstable and emerging locations, Newmont was high on our list for recruitment as another potential multinational corporate partner for Business on the Frontlines.

Just weeks after our visit to GE, we traveled to Denver to interview Newmont's CEO, Wayne Murdy. Tall, thoughtful, and soft spoken, Murdy came from a humble South Dakota farm family and was an accounting partner at Arthur Andersen before transitioning into a career as a mining executive. At Newmont's corporate headquarters, we stepped into certainly the fanciest and probably the most expensive elevator we'd ever entered. Valuable minerals and stones—green malachite, red and white marble—covered each wall. The whole corporate headquarters exuded power and affluence.

Mining in general, and gold mining in particular, takes a lot of nerve. It is the equivalent of going all in on a hand of poker. Companies bet amounts that approach a billion dollars on each mine. But unlike poker, they don't know for decades whether the investment will pay off. It isn't like drilling for oil when you know fairly quickly whether you hit the jackpot. When you mine for gold, getting results can take up to twenty years. Mining exploration licenses frequently cover vast territories equivalent to the size of Bulgaria or Cuba. Additionally, rich veins of minerals are often found in politically unstable regions of the globe, locations with minimal infrastructure, electricity, and communications.

Despite often remote locations and challenging conditions, these aren't the low-tech coal mines of the olden days that relied on endless streams of manual labor. Multinational mining companies are sophisticated operations, requiring engineers, surveyors, and other highly trained professionals to operate the high-tech machinery and equipment in the mines and metallurgy plants. Companies invest hundreds of millions of dollars in building their own roads and cell towers. Crushing tons of ore into ounces of minerals requires massive amounts of electrical power. At one site, Murdy told us, Newmont planned to use hydroelectric power, but then the country suffered a hundred-year drought. They had to purchase a floating electricity plant in Houston, sail it across the Atlantic Ocean, and dock it off the coast of West Africa to produce the power their mining operations needed. Mines must earn a return acceptable to shareholders, all while accounting for a wide range of unexpected costs, including natural disasters, corruption and even the risk of takeover by a host government looking to nationalize assets. If mineral prices collapse and mines are forced to shutter, capital expenditures become sunk costs, and all this investment is lost.

We asked Murdy the same question we had asked Taylor, wanting to hear about his most difficult business decision. After some reflection, Murdy responded, "The gold mine in Ahafo." In 2003, Newmont opened what would ultimately become the world's largest gold mine, in Ahafo, Ghana. This mine embodied all of the things that make mining such a risky enterprise. The prospecting license covered thousands of square miles, and the mine itself covered hundreds of square miles—an area nearly the size of Los Angeles. Newmont's initial investment was $350 million, more than six times the total foreign direct investment in all of Ghana in the previous year.[1] The part of the Brong-Ahafo region where the mine was located offered very few access roads, limited electricity, and almost no telecommunication.

We asked, "Why Ghana?"

Murdy paused, considered whether his words would be taken the wrong way, and then said them anyway. "Well, because it's Africa for beginners," he replied.

We knew the sociopolitical conditions to which he referred. Unlike many of its neighbors, Ghana was stable and democratic. Since its independence from Great Britain in 1957, it had consistent peaceful transitions of power between parties in the government, a navigable legal and regulatory framework, and a relatively educated workforce. However, we also knew that North and West Africa was a region that had the potential to be a hotbed of conflict.[2]

We asked how Newmont handled security challenges, expecting to hear about vulnerability assessment, levels of contingency planning, and exit strategies. However, Murdy's answer was light years away from Taylor's calculated approach.

"The only way to protect the mine is if the community perceives that this is their mine and they protect it," he told us. "You cannot hire enough security in isolated places. If an angry mob wants to overrun the mine, they will overrun and take over the mine. There is nothing you can do."

Murdy described a number of policies that helped generate community buy-in: Training highly paid local engineers and managers and hiring an entirely local staff. Buying food, uniforms, and housing from local suppliers. Bringing electricity and building roads where there were none. Establishing a charitable foundation to give back a portion of profits, with a local board of elders who decided where the money was to be spent.

Both Taylor and Murdy were so thoughtful and measured in their approach to security in unstable regions, yet the two men had come to opposite conclusions about how to protect the millions of dollars of investment. Both had the well-being of their employees, shareholders, and broader stakeholders in mind. And both were incredibly successful implementing their approach. Taylor would essentially build a wall as high as needed to protect the company's investments. Murdy believed you could never build a wall high enough, so he found ways to make sure that the community was invested in the company's success.

We found ourselves pondering how these vastly different approaches would compare in other frontline situations. Which one should a company use to secure its investments? A few years later we got the chance to put this question to the test.

Putting Our Ideas Regarding Security in the Frontlines to the Test

Our friend Lieutenant General Charlie Cleveland had developed his own perspectives regarding security. As the US Army Special Operations Commander, Cleveland recognized the value of and prioritized military-civilian collaboration on national security objectives. After the success of our deployment to Senegal as described in our Introduction, he supported another mission to develop and test new collaboration mechanisms between the military and business. We convened an even more diverse team of professors, professionals, and soldiers from all three parts of USASOC—Special Forces, Civil Affairs, and Psychological Operations—and turned our focus to the problems facing Honduras.

With its drug cartels and lucrative gang-run operations, Honduras had become one of the most violent places in the world. In 2014,

San Pedro Sula's civilian murder rate was the highest in the world, at 187 per 100,000. The next-worst place was Baghdad, where most of the soldiers had been deployed during the height of the US Army surge in 2007, its murder rate was 89 per 100,000.[3] US naval operations during the previous decade had successfully interrupted drug trafficking in the Caribbean, but this had pushed narco-traffickers to adopt strategic land routes through Nicaragua, Honduras, Guatemala, and Mexico.[4] That change increased gang violence in our target area, the neighborhood of Chamelecón in the city of San Pedro Sula, and created instability in related areas, including the nearby agricultural region of the Aguan River Valley. These two places found themselves in the geographic crosshairs—narco-traffickers essentially made the Aguan Valley into a drug superhighway, with Colombian and Mexican cartels meeting in the middle in San Pedro Sula. Our joint mission was to encourage the launch and expansion of businesses whose sustained presence could provide the means and motivation for young Hondurans to eschew illegal activities like gang violence and drug trafficking.

The work we did to prepare for Honduras, what we call "pre-mission prep," was very different from our usual work with communities, companies, and NGOs. We quickly realized that not only were there deep differences between the military and civilian arms of our team, but that the soldiers themselves came from three different branches of USASOC that were unaccustomed to collaboration. Simple things, like soliciting dissenting opinions, proved challenging as our more junior soldiers deferred to the officers in the group and the Special Forces soldiers often dominated discussions.

Although we had learned a lot in Senegal, the team had to start from scratch, working together to build a shared culture and a common vocabulary. Eventually, the civilians came to use terms that were more common in the military world, like "adversary" and "threat," and the soldiers became more comfortable with words that were more typical to business, like "opportunity" and "market." Our civilian contingent learned to consider security threats more closely, while the soldiers learned to think about the critical importance of jobs, especially for young men as an alternative to gang life. Soldiers immersed themselves in introductory finance, accounting, operations, and marketing, as well as international law and peace studies. Civilians poured through military strategy and doctrine.

Next, we tested our new security and business problem-solving collaboration by sending our joint team into two of the most dynamic, difficult, and opposite contexts we could imagine. First, we all traveled to Silicon Valley to design and launch e-commerce businesses and pitch them to venture capitalists. Next, we arranged to spend time with Honduran gang members incarcerated in the Los Angeles County Jail, to consider strategies for reducing recidivism. Both experiences provided our team new insights and helped us get ready to work together to find actionable business solutions to the security threats in Honduras. Lieutenant General Cleveland's superior, and another of our advocates, four-star General John Kelly, sent us on our way, in his usual gruff manner, reminding us to keep an open mind and essentially permitting us to diverge from the normal military playbook: "You just can't shoot your way out of some of these problems."

Unlike our Senegal deployment, Honduras posed more acute security risks. The civilians on our team, who were accustomed to wandering freely, were eager to get out in the cities, markets, and countryside and talk to local people directly. However, this made the military members of our team deeply uncomfortable. They seemed to be always on guard. We sometimes thought their wariness was overblown, and we even joked about the predictability of their seating choices in restaurants—always with their backs to the wall facing the exit. But in San Pedro Sula the telling signs of the potential for violence lurked around every corner. For example, the civilians never would have identified a man sitting on a folding chair at the top of a hill as a threat. But our teammates quickly pointed out his hidden weapon and deliberate positioning with a clear line of sight to a square below. In the Chamelecón section of San Pedro Sula, we stood on the street that separated the territories of MS-16 and Barrio 18, two of the biggest Honduran gangs. Our military teammates could translate the competing graffiti splashed along the walls of stores and houses marking each gang's territory. Eerily, the street was deserted. No bikes, motorcycles, or cars. No pedestrians, street vendors, residents sitting on porches, or kids playing soccer in the street—all of which were commonplace in the rest of overpopulated, frenetic San Pedro Sula. We swiftly exited.

Despite the violence in Chamelecón and the Aguan Valley, local businessmen and expatriate Hondurans in Miami described to our teammates exciting business prospects in textile and electronics manufacturing, food processing, server farms, and call centers. The advantages were straightforward—many Hondurans are bilingual, shipping to the East Coast of the United States is fast and easy, and the country is in a time zone compatible with business in North America. But to take advantage of these opportunities, any business looking to operate in Honduras would have to mitigate the significant security risks.

The situation in Honduras was a perfect illustration of one of the most difficult challenges for business in frontline economies. Businesses could contribute to stability and provide economic alternatives to drug smuggling and gangs, but the region needed to improve security first to attract investment. Taking General Taylor's approach at

GE, viewing security as a fixed cost, we struggled to make the business case work. Unfortunately, the investment based on GE's protocols to keep personnel and property safe made the math impossible, as it would erode most of the potential profits from those opportunities. Year after year, as business investment passed over Honduras for more stable alternative regions, gangs deepened their strongholds, making subsequent investment even less likely. It was obvious to us why GE's presence in Honduras was largely as a consumer brand rather than as a producer or employer.[5] As one potential investor, a textile manufacturer who had more than enough demand to expand his operations in San Pedro Sula, put it, "Why make significant additional investments when all of the profits will likely be extorted by the gangs?"[6]

GE's approach was a nonstarter, but we found a great deal of promise in embracing Murdy's approach at Newmont Mining. Thinking of security as a variable rather than a fixed cost, we projected the initial steps of business investments and then forecast their potential security implications. We modeled a number of incremental investments using targeted (and in this case, collaborative) policies and activities aimed at reinforcing the combination of security, governance, and business. In San Pedro Sula, we observed that dozens of individuals and small organizations were already in fact working with a similar aim of improving livelihoods. However, working independently, they didn't create enough impact to disrupt the cycle of violence or to substantively grow economic activity. Emerging data from local interviews indicated a possible path forward for stabilizing the area and making long-term business opportunities more attractive. For this to happen, though, these largely unconnected initiatives needed to be knit together into a more coordinated effort focused on a single territory to have a chance of taking control back from the gangs.[7]

Our team developed a coordinating process built around the efforts of many like-minded Hondurans—seamstresses, priests, grandmothers, small business owners—who shared our interest in stabilizing the region, taking it back from gang control. Becoming troubleshooters, we identified obstacles to economic growth and investment and then worked with a wide range of actors, like the municipal government, local businesses, and NGOs, to design ways to overcome them. For example, our team partnered with local Honduran organizations, including a vocational school, to expand job training and then coordinate the local market for labor, with the goal of facilitating the private sector to hire skilled young people for legitimate employment. Our overall objective was to kick-start sufficient momentum to inspire those businesses who were already inclined to invest to make the decision to do so. Once it took on a momentum of its own, other business, community, and municipal leaders dove in to drive the process further.

We adopted Newmont's strategy of spending locally and actively encouraged targeted investments to strengthen security. For instance, the San Pedro Sula police force desperately needed training and supplies. Our soldiers quickly organized the training, but the police also needed new uniforms to make officers visible and identifiable when out patrolling the streets. Sophisticated training and brand-new uniforms would also instill pride in this once demoralized force. A soldier on our team immediately thought that he might be able to leverage the US Army's procurement process to get the new uniforms at a discount, and he picked up the phone and got a quote from the 7th Special Forces Group headquarters in Florida. We quickly realized that, although efficient, this solution missed an opportunity. Honduras has a long-standing textile industry, with skilled tailors and seamstresses producing low-cost apparel for the US market. Why not purchase the new police uniforms locally? We always try to purchase from local producers as much as possible to provide opportunities for local businesses to build up resilience and strength, which in turn further enhances stability in their communities.

We pivoted to place a large order for new police uniforms with a local seamstress association. This purchase order provided sufficient revenue for them to invest in more sewing machines, enabling them to hire and train more seamstresses. The process of fulfilling a large order on time and at cost taught the association about bidding for larger outsourcing contracts from American apparel retailers, a helpful lesson for handling future growth. With the funds from this order, this association also purchased a small building on the edge of Chamelecón and began running some of their operations from there.

However, despite this early positive momentum, the path of transforming the local conditions from the ground up was neither straight nor smooth. Even the seamstresses faced setbacks, as some larger customers canceled their orders because of changing economic circumstances, while others did not pay up on time. Building businesses in the frontlines is not without its hurdles. Nonetheless, the persistent coordinated efforts of multiple local organizations, businesses, and professions all pulling together kept the momentum going. In the end, the seamstresses moving into their new building symbolized their optimism for the future, a signal that other local businesses took to heart in making investment plans. Acquiring new uniforms for the police force didn't just build morale for the cops; by following our principle of buying local, additional community members benefited, and the neighborhood took small steps forward.

Outside the city, along the northern coast, our team was working on the instability caused by the wholesale collapse of the major regional industry: palm oil production. In recent years, plantations in Indonesia and Malaysia were the largest producers of palm oil, with 85 percent of the global market. To address domestic policy priorities, Indonesia began heavily subsidizing domestic consumers, as the poor used palm oil for cooking. Enterprising exporters then bought large quantities of cheap Indonesian local palm oil to resell on the global markets, thereby triggering the sharp fall of the global price of this commodity.[8] Because of policy decisions made by the Indonesian government to address domestic priorities on the other side of the world, the predominant economic sector in this corner of Honduras was decimated. What we found was that those palm oil farmers, without suitable economic alternatives, turned to the narco-traffickers for work and allowed them to traverse their now abandoned palm oil plantations to smuggle drugs. We thought we could work with the farmers to diversify their crops and find new markets for their produce. We also got lucky. This area possessed a useful underutilized asset: a natural deep-water port in Trujillo that would be ideal for the transportation of both people and goods if security could be improved. We identified opportunities for crop exports, helped form local farmer's cooperatives, and used our connections to incentivize US agricultural multinationals to broker export agreements. With this legitimate income, farmers would be more likely to resist the traffickers, who in turn would be forced to take other transportation routes.

As the security situation improved, other uses of the port would become more viable. For example, we worked with local tourism organizations to develop new initiatives, including the potential arrival of cruise ships. Our group text exploded with cheers when it was announced in 2016 that Royal Caribbean and Seabourn Quest luxury cruises were going to start docking at the port of Trujillo at the end of the Aguan Valley to introduce tourists to this historic, beautiful, and overlooked corner of the Caribbean where Columbus landed in 1502.

Through this organic, multifaceted, but relatively coordinated process, local Honduran business owners, expatriate investors, municipal and community leaders, US Special Forces, and local police improved the security situation in San Pedro Sula and the northern coast. Although it was a modest change, it was sufficient to trigger further business investment even after our team completed our deployment. To illustrate, other direct foreign investment leaned into the Honduran economy's comparative advantages. Its bilingual, low-cost labor force located in a similar time zone as the US provided opportunities for call centers and business-process outsourcing. In 2019, the Denver-based business process company Startek began to offer outsourcing services to American Fortune 500 companies with a $22 million investment in a delivery campus and call center in San Pedro Sula. Since 2019, more than 2,200 employees now support these customer-service operations.

Given San Pedro Sula's strategic location on the highways leading from Mexico down Central America, our team investigated opportunities in manufacturing, logistics, and warehousing, which later came to fruition. In 2018, Texas Armoring Corporation, the world's leading producer of premium armored commercial vehicles and bulletproof cars, invested $230 million in a vehicle armoring plant in San Pedro Sula. Around the same time, Nike expanded its operation beyond its existing seven sportswear and shoe factories in San Pedro Sula by opening its first $40 million logistics center, which it expects to turn into another production facility as well creating an estimated twenty-five thousand employees over time. As Nike's first logistics center in Latin America, it executes fulfillments across Central America and the United States. To address the need for reliable power in Honduras, SunEdison and other course, the local Hondurans on the ground who were taking the risks and embarking on new business ventures were the lynchpin in this progress.

Turning Security into a Variable Cost Opens Up Options for Expansion

Conventional wisdom holds that operating in unstable frontline environments is cost prohibitive and thus should be avoided. The expenses of employee protection, extortion, and unpredictable shutdowns can make expansion into an insecure market seem impossible at first glance. But in Honduras, our experience showed that this need not be the case. There is another mindset that can help businesses take advantage of these untapped opportunities. Most executives perceive security as a fixed cost, something that rises to their attention only when considering doomsday scenarios like needing to evacuate expats during a crisis or developing work stoppage guidelines with suppliers. If they do expand into the frontlines, this mindset leads companies to make heavy upfront infrastructure investments that would take many years to pay back, even under the best of circumstances.

However, through the strategies outlined in this chapter that lead to greater embeddedness in the local community, businesses can turn high fixed security costs into variable costs. And if those same decisions could reduce security costs over time, this would essentially break down a significant decision—whether to expand into a frontline environment—into a series of smaller ones. Seeing security as a variable cost enables incremental, small-scale investment in frontline environments, permitting businesses to test the waters, gather valuable information, and adjust to changing circumstances as needed. Businesses gain much-needed flexibility in how to execute overseas expansions.

What our team found both in the Aguan Valley and in San Pedro Sula was that the risk-return scales needed to be tipped only modestly, through embracing policies that gradually reduced security costs, to encourage investors already contemplating new business launches to make the required investments. Even if they aren't teaming up with the military like we did, companies can look for ways to shore up other parts of the region's security systems through, for example, building relationships with a wide spectrum of respected local leaders and engaging with local communities. Those who do the creative thinking and hard work of building local relationships will earn the first-mover advantages.

Security costs don't have to stay high and fixed. Pragmatic local policies that combine an emphasis on the common good with profit can help companies operate more securely in frontline markets. Business partnerships really can help stabilize formerly violent regions. Most importantly, the way these lessons played out in parts of Honduras showed how business can simultaneously thrive and make investments that then enable the campesinos in the Aguan Valley and the seamstresses and other small business proprietors in San Pedro Sula to thrive as well.

Our team knew we were winning when gang leaders began quietly sending their own younger brothers and older sons to the local businesses our team helped launch for jobs. Even though the gang leaders themselves may not be able to escape gang life, those jobs represented new possibilities and a way out for their families.

Earning a reasonable payback on investments in frontline environments certainly depends on cautiously managing upfront capital outlays and ongoing costs. Deeply embedding operations into communities encourages both stability and security, as locals begin to protect the business because they perceive its success to be their own. In addition, investment in the frontlines also opens up exciting opportunities to reach new sources of supply and natural resources. Often, their sheer inaccessibility makes these resources particularly valuable. How can businesses consistently and reliably gain entry into such difficult places? The following chapter explores strategies that enable businesses to access such new resources, while mitigating the inevitable vulnerabilities in their supply chains. These strategies can provide low-cost supplies for companies while simultaneously improving the lives and livelihoods of the poor.

CHAPTER 3

Savvy Supply Chains

Rethinking supply chains can provide low-cost solutions for business while simultaneously improving the lives of small-scale producers.

You want us to get this where?!" exclaimed Holly, one of our business students who is now an executive at United Airlines, as she peered down the side of a mountain cliff with twenty pounds of coffee in her backpack destined for Green Mountain Coffee Roasters. High-quality coffee grows on the sides of the steep mountains of Guatemala where volcanic soil provides the perfect balance of nutrients. Some of the world's best coffee is grown in inaccessible locations in East Africa and South and Central America. To make a pound of coffee, it takes two thousand bright red cherries, each of which contains two beans. Once the beans are picked, they must be transported to a processing facility where the cherries are crushed to remove the skins and pulp. The beans are then left to ferment before washing, drying, and sorting by quality. With an average weight of fifteen grams per cherry, Holly would have to trek up and down that hill four times to produce a single twelve-ounce bag of coffee. Every one of Green Mountain Coffee Roasters beans takes a similar journey, from a small farm perched on the side of a mountain all the way to your morning cup.

On that hill, we also saw how coffee and bananas make wonderful companions. Intercropping creates a natural symbiosis. Banana trees create shade for the sun-sensitive coffee while not competing for water as much as shade trees do. Studies that compare the yield of mono-cropped coffee plots with intercropped banana-coffee plots demonstrate that the coffee yield remains the same while simultaneously the bananas increase food security, supplement nutrition, and provide an additional source of income for farmers.[1] We were in Guatemala to work with one of Green Mountain Coffee's suppliers, a small cooperative, to figure out how to realize that additional income from bananas. To sell the bananas, the farmers would have to transport them down the steep mountainside paths for pickup on the road below. As Holly started down the hill, she exclaimed, "Coffee, maybe. Bananas, no way!"

The next day we traveled from the mountains to the plateau near the capital city to investigate an alternative way to get bananas to market in Guatemala. We parked our car in a gated parking lot and were met by the facility's manager. We walked around the brick building and saw row upon row of equally spaced, perfectly pruned banana plants. As we got closer, we saw a conveyor belt with shiny stainless-steel rollers snaking between the rows of plants. Workers in uniforms gently placed impeccable bunches of bananas on the conveyor belts to be transported to other employees inside the building who were packing crates for export. Even the dirt paths appeared spotless. This efficient mass pro-duction seemed generations away from the disarray of the village next door, with its clucking chickens and families cooking meals over fires in their thatched-roof homes. Welcome to the Dole company-owned banana plantation just outside Guatemala City.

Supply Chain Dilemma: Make or Buy

The supply chain for a product can be thought of as the journey of interconnected steps that raw materials and other components take as they are processed or assembled into the end products for sale to customers. Supply chains are all about getting physical things sourced, manufactured, and transported inexpensively, quickly, and correctly. The term "value chain" broadens business decisions beyond the physical supply chain to include activities such as research, product design, and marketing and advertising to drive demand. In this chapter, we focus mainly on different approaches to acquiring raw materials in frontline environments through improving resilience and lowering the cost of physical supply chains. Accessing these raw materials represents the gateway to frontline environments and often opens up increasingly sophisticated investment opportunities.

When any link in the supply chain is not working properly, the disruption can impact the bottom line both through extra expenses and loss of revenues. Resilience in supply chains means that business maintains multiple robust sources of supply or extra production capacity to accommodate shifts in demand or overcome interruptions without compromising quality. Many food companies, whether processors or supermarkets, have been wary of establishing sourcing arrangements in frontline markets based on worries about resilience. When they contemplate supply from such markets, they are more likely to follow the Dole model, wholly-owned modern facilities near an urban area, than the Green Mountain Coffee model, which involves working with thousands of small farmers and hundreds of traders.

The lens of classic economic theory can help shed light on such tough judgment calls. Theory posits that business activities are organized either within the control of a company or via transactions of buying and selling in a marketplace, depending on which situation lowers costs at reasonable risk. In the decision of "make versus buy," if communication, transaction, and interaction costs to buy goods and services consistently and reliably in the marketplace are too high, then firms will bring them in house and conduct more business activities within their sphere of control, essentially doing those activities themselves. However, if the alternative is cheaper, then a company will buy what it needs in the market from other suppliers.[2]

Navigating the uncertainty of supply chains in faraway places, like the mountains in Guatemala, has largely been the domain of supply chain researchers and practitioners. The theory of supply chain resilience posits that there must be a balance between supply vulnerabilities and an organization's internal capacity to mitigate those vulnerabilities.[3] Supply vulnerabilities could be any type of supply interruption or logistics problems, like disruptions with shipping carriers and their schedules or difficulty sourcing raw materials. Investment in IT and tracking systems can help a firm mitigate those vulnerabilities. A track-and-trace system across multiple plants can follow raw materials through the process of becoming finished goods. Should inputs be delayed from one supplier, company managers can decide to reroute other sources of raw materials to the plants most urgently in need of them, preventing costly operational shutdowns. How a firm navigates that balance increases their resilience to supply disruptions and ultimately drives their profitability.

Given the many uncertainties associated with doing business in frontline environments, making the initial large capital outlays and running the operations to control supply rather than face ongoing unpredictability can be a prudent approach as long as the opportunity is large enough to generate sufficient returns at acceptable risk levels. It's reasonable to worry about local supply. Smallholder farmers often struggle to meet the exacting standards of timing, reliability, and quality dictated by large buyers. They require support through education and technology, as well as access to high-quality inputs such as seeds, pesticides, and fertilizers, not to mention dependable transportation across difficult and sometimes dangerous terrain. Further, the average size of a farm in the global south is less than 2 hectares, as compared with the average US farm of 180 hectares.[4] To source enough volume, companies would be forced to negotiate with hundreds or even thousands of small farmers. The sheer number of suppliers and the differences in their capabilities and farming techniques are likely to produce variability in quality that is challenging to manage. From this perspective, it is no wonder that Dole became one of the largest landowners in Guatemala and chose to plant its own banana plantations and build its own processing facilities rather than accept the uncertainty of sourcing from hundreds of small farms. Companies like Dole often view these significant upfront investments as a necessary step to mitigate uncertainty. However, Dole's strategy is no magic bullet. The prospect of buying land, importing equipment, building and staffing facilities, and continuing to operate in the middle of the jungle in a politically volatile country can be daunting. This is an expensive approach, justified for only the largest companies and the most attractive opportunities.

Within just a few miles of each other in Guatemala, Dole and Green Mountain Coffee Roasters have solved the problems of make versus buy with supply chains extending into frontline environments. Like GE's approach to security, this approach is effective, but it is also expensive and out of reach for all but the largest corporations when expanding into smaller frontline markets.

The Green Mountain Coffee Approach

Green Mountain Coffee Roasters opened its doors in 1993 with a mission to purchase only coffee that is grown in a way that conserves nature. Over time, its mission expanded to prioritize improving the lives of those who grow and process the coffee. Green Mountain Coffee's broad on-the-ground relationships with multiple untraditional allies mitigate supply risks and serve as the foundation of its supply chain model. At the center of this strategy lies their long-term relations with local traders, whom the company monitors closely for their commitment to act as trusted intermediaries between themselves and the small coffee farmers. Green Mountain Coffee also partners broadly with NGOs like Catholic Relief Services and Root Capital to build the infrastructure for training farmers on sustainable farming and processing practices, negotiating long-term supply commitments, and providing targeted financing and investment.

This model has been extremely successful. In 2022, Green Mountain Coffee bought more than 125,000 metric tons of sustainably sourced coffee from traders and small farmers around the world. To put this into perspective, a ten-foot-tall adult elephant weighs approximately 1 metric ton. Although still a small portion of the overall global coffee market, Green Mountain Coffee is now the prime purchaser of coffee beans for their own brands, like Donut Shop, but also for large customers like McDonalds. Despite its smaller overall global market share, Green Mountain Coffee has established the environmental sustainability standard that much larger companies are now following, according to external audits by Fairtrade and the Rainforest Alliance.[8] In 2020, Green Mountain Coffee reached one of their goals—100 percent of the coffee they purchased was sustainably grown.

Green Mountain Coffee is able to choose to buy in the make versus buy supply chain decision because they mitigate their supply chain vulnerabilities by aligning with a network of trusted partners to support small coffee farmers. By deeply embedding their staff in communities of coffee growers, they are able to discern the trustworthiness of local traders, working with only those who provide needed services to coffee growers and canceling contracts with those who may exploit their market power, like the armed middlemen we encountered in rural Western Uganda in Chapter 1. Green Mountain Coffee further works in multiple geographies across the world to ensure that weather or civil unrest does not threaten their entire supply. They provide farmers with seeds, training, and fertilizer to help facilitate consistent quality. They often guarantee a price floor to ensure that farmers will sell to them rather than competitors. As one of Green Mountain Coffee's executives succinctly stated in an interview with us, "We treat our farmers better, our traders treat our farmers better, and then our supply of coffee is more stable and resilient."

Green Mountain Coffee's partnerships are a key part of their success. Through their relationship with World Coffee Research, a nonprofit agricultural research lab, they support the cultivation of new coffee varieties that can both withstand the negative effects of climate change and increase yields for farmers. They paired with Root Capital, a financial nonprofit, to support financing, long-term loans, and management training for hundreds of coffee cooperatives around the world. Through the Blue Harvest partnership with Catholic Relief Services in Central America, they also support workshops for thousands of farmers on water-conservation practices and restoring watersheds and water systems. This knowledge is essential both for coffee farms to flourish and for the health of the downstream communities.[9] Finally, they support the efforts of local NGOs to assist farmers to achieve Fair Trade certification, which earns them better prices for their coffee. They collaborate with the many different organizations supporting the millions of farmers in this last mile of the supply chain, so neither Green Mountain Coffee nor the farmers themselves need to absorb all the tasks and all the responsibility. Through these strategic partnerships, Green Mountain Coffee and its small-scale farmers benefit from increased research and development. Moreover, conducting business in a sustainable way is not only consistent with its core operating principles but also makes Green Mountain Coffee more attractive to consumers. These are business advantages that they could not achieve on their own.

Our experience in the frontlines leads us to believe that this approach is not only viable for companies with high-margin products like coffee. Other firms work with small growers to source their ingredients. As described in Chapter 1, the largest fast food restaurant in the Philippines, Jollibee, built an outreach program to support small farmers so that it could acquire enough supply of onions and other vegetables to fulfill their domestic customers' growing demands. These relationships became so strategically important that Jollibee further invested in its ongoing Farmer Entrepreneurship Program to help its small-scale suppliers sustain their modest livelihoods during the COVID-19 pandemic.

Creating Savvy Supply Chains in the Amazon

The sheer humidity of the Brazilian rainforest made it tough going for our boat to travel up the Amazon. Flowering plants grew on top of shrubs, on top of palms, filling our lungs with oxygen, moisture, and energy. The traditional communities whose homes on stilts cling to the Amazon River banks call themselves "the children of the forest." They see it as their responsibility to protect one of the world's most important ecosystems. When we ask about travel by riverboat from their homesteads to the closest market town, they answer in days rather than hours. Any products harvested from the rainforest must travel more than two thousand miles along the Amazon River to the major regional city of Manaus.

The Amazon is filled with rich natural treasures, such as acai, cassava, guarana, and other jungle fruits and vegetables. In addition to the sheer distance to market, there are many other challenges to commercializing these resources. Communities on the river are sparse, frequently hours apart, making collection and transportation of goods to market towns costly. Cell phone coverage is extremely limited, impeding communication between the river communities and potential outside customers. Few of the people who live on the river have more than a primary education, leaving these communities further isolated. The only electricity comes from the occasional diesel generator. Because people rarely migrate from these outlying areas into urban centers, there are few existing relations upon which to build trust to facilitate business transactions.

The Amazon is a classic frontline environment. Communities are constantly facing incursion from marauders and ranchers looking to capitalize on the land's productivity. There is no rule of law, except what the river communities themselves can enforce. Most families live on thirteen dollars per month obtained through the direct financial assistance program called the Bolsa Floresta that the state of Amazonas pays residents to protect the forest.[10] Despite the richness of the land, the heavy transportation costs for boats and the diesel needed to power them would likely tip any commercial venture into unprofitability. There is a good reason why few outsiders have even attempted to create a supply chain here.

The Fundação Amazonas Sustentável (FAS), or Foundation for Amazon Sustainability, founded in 2008, is considered the voice of the Amazon. As the leading environmental NGO in Brazil, it has launched conservation efforts, advocated for improved ecological protection of the forest, and even supported efforts that brought a number of species of birds, animals, and fish back from the brink of extinction. Building on its success as a conservation organization, FAS reached out to us in 2017 for assistance in balancing environmental imperatives with the economic needs of the traditional river communities. We describe our joint goal as "making the forest worth more standing up than cut down."[11] We believe that by commercializing the products found in their forest, communities could determine how to use those natural resources sustainably and according to their conservationist values, while simultaneously leveraging their intimate knowledge of the forest to keep out less sustainably minded competitors.

Our collaboration started by exploring the commercial possibilities surrounding the pirarucu, a three-hundred-pound prehistoric air-breathing dinosaur fish that is considered a Brazilian delicacy. The people who live in the Mamiraua and Uacari Reserves in the Amazon don't actually fish for this beast; they hunt it. When the waters recede for two months each fall, fishermen stand in their narrow kayaks and harpoon the pirarucu from fifty feet away when it comes up to the surface to take a breath. It takes the effort of the whole community—the men, women and children—to clean the fish and carry it from the lakes to the river for transport to urban customers.

Interviews with fish processors and supermarkets in Manaus, Rio de Janeiro, and São Paulo convinced us that a large and stable market demand existed for pirarucu. Almost every Brazilian family prepares a pirarucu dish during Semana Santa, the Holy Week between Palm Sunday and Easter. The communities could easily sell every pirarucu that they could catch. The question, then, was not about demand; the question was how to deliver the supply of pirarucu to these faraway customers at a reasonable cost.

The communities needed transportation—and the only transport available in the Amazon was boats. And they needed big boats with specially designed refrigerated holds to keep the pirarucu fresh along their thousand-mile journey to Manaus. No one community could embark on such an endeavor on its own. To achieve the necessary economies of scale, we organized eight hundred fishing families across fifty communities into eight associations. We then helped arrange a modest initial investment: the associations purchased eight boats, allowing the communities to bypass exploitative middlemen who abused their monopoly power and paid very low prices. With their new boats, the fishermen would take their pirarucu catch directly to the large food processors and urban customers to earn better prices. The associations purchased two cold storage facilities, which enabled them to store the fish from the end of the fishing season in November until Holy Week the following year, when the price for pirarucu was much higher. FAS staff helped broker the initial customer relationships in Manaus, which led to purchase contracts.

Even with all these details accounted for, it took several years of effort to establish a reliable supply chain. In the first year, our team spent weeks going up and down the river with FAS staff, sleeping in hammocks on boats, visiting with local leaders to explain the commercialization opportunities for their communities. This initiative would have been impossible without the considerable social capital earned over time by local FAS staff, who had built trust through their enduring presence in the Amazon. FAS staff built this trust by assisting the river communities with education and healthcare in addition to its core mission of conservation. It was their long history with the communities that enabled FAS staff to support the initial launch of the new fishing associations.

At the beginning of this venture, nevertheless, our team suffered months of sleepless nights. Given our experience with the response of the armed middlemen in Western Uganda to our new market arrangements a few years earlier, we worried about how the powerful middlemen in the Amazon would react. In the remote rainforest with minimal formal rule of law, a few thugs with axes late at night could certainly sink the eight new boats and our entire plan. Fortunately, because the middlemen lost only a small fraction of their overall business along the Amazon due to loss of pirarucu sales, the river communities did not suffer the feared reprisals.

During the first fishing season, the families in the participating river communities increased their incomes by nearly 30 percent, mainly through earning higher prices for the pirarucu they caught.[12] Within three years, they had recouped their investment on purchase of the boats. Many families used the extra money to send at least one of their children to live with friends and family in the market towns so that they could attend secondary school. The fish processors and supermarkets now had a dedicated supply of pirarucu.

In the subsequent years, we have continued to collaborate with FAS to commercialize other resources from the jungle, like guarana. This bright red berry has more caffeine per ounce than coffee and has become a popular ingredient in energy drinks around the world. At harvest time in November, in the Maués Reserve in the Amazon, the red berries pop open to reveal white pulp and black seeds that look like either thousands of curious eyes, on a good day, or a creepy Halloween nightmare, on a bad one. Locals pick the berries then slowly toast the seeds in enormous frying pans over open fires before hand-grinding them into a fine powder, which can be dissolved in water.

To access larger market opportunities, the farmers first needed to improve their harvesting techniques to enhance product quality. FAS organized and provided this critical training. We also worked with FAS and the local guarana harvesters in Maués to build a very simple processing plant to transform the berries into powder in a way that guaranteed quality control and maintained consistent caffeine content and taste profiles. After these needed improvements, when it came time to negotiate contracts with big customers, FAS was a trusted intermediary. AmBev, a Brazilian beverage company now owned by Anheuser-Busch, buys most of the guarana produced in the Maués Reserve to make the top-selling drink in Brazil called Guaraná Antarctica. Through this multiyear collaboration between small-scale producers, the local NGO, and the multinational corporation, the families harvesting guarana have nearly doubled their incomes, from about R$2,000 to nearly R$4,000 per household.[13] Without the steady supply of guarana harvested by the Maués communities, AmBev would be unable to bring the Guaraná Antarctica brand to the world.[14]

The Future Will Demand More Savvy Supply Chains

From mountainsides to factories, to manufacturers and markets, the movement of products around the world is a challenge that goes hand in hand with globalization. It is only recently that rising food prices and empty supermarket shelves caused by the COVID pandemic and the war in Ukraine brought the topic of supply chain fragility to Western dinner tables. However, this problem is likely here to stay. The combination of population growth and rising prosperity is increasing the demand for food. In fact, the World Bank estimates that demand for food will double by 2050.[15] At the same time, the amount of agricultural land is decreasing owing to urbanization and the consequences of poor land management. The pressure to use high-quality agricultural land to produce biofuels as more sustainable energy sources further exacerbates this situation.[16] Globalizing the food system, particularly by improving the productivity and accessibility of agriculture in frontline environments, is one important path to sufficient food production. However, simply transplanting plantations across the globe, in the tradition of Dole, will not represent a sustainable solution for food security. In addition to displacing the most vulnerable populations, these large-scale farms are acutely susceptible to risk from adverse climate events such as droughts and floods and political unrest. Instead, scholars and practitioners alike suggest that we will need to source more of our food from where it can grow naturally.[17]

Green Mountain Coffee has shown that it is possible to build a profitable business in a way that embodies a diverse and distributed globalized food supply based on multiple local partnerships with nontraditional allies and sourcing from thousands of small-holder farmers. They consistently and reliably achieve high quality. Our experience shows that this is a viable alternative to the Dole model of extensive (and expensive) vertical integration. With reasonable risk mitigation, businesses can develop what we call *savvy supply chains* that lower the significant upfront capital outlays while simultaneously improving the lives of small-scale farmers, fishermen, and producers. Green Mountain Coffee executives quite candidly and publicly credit their success to their dedicated coffee growers around the world, which the company has supported through sensitive policies that address their needs. Our own work in the Amazon demonstrates that there are real advantages to accessing remote sources of supply.

To capture these opportunities, businesses will need long-term vision, patience, and ongoing trouble shooting to develop savvy supply chains. To succeed in the frontlines, businesses will also need new skills to identify, develop, and manage multiple nontraditional partnerships with NGOs and other organizations that support small producers. This collaborative effort, then, can generate both competitive advantage for the business and benefits for the small farmer. Even modest investment in small local producers, such as technical assistance, access to credit, and management training, builds irreplaceable goodwill and loyalty on both sides. Because most frontline markets do not have the scale to warrant significant upfront investments, this approach enables both businesses and their local partners to work together, learn from their mistakes, and then scale over time.

And thus, it's a win for business as this approach allows companies to enter into these markets more cautiously. It's a win for consumers who want these products. And it's a win for local communities because such collaborations jump-start the flywheel of inclusive rural economic development that will go a long way to breaking the cycle of poverty in the frontlines.

Underpinning the business case lies the magnitude of underdeveloped frontline opportunity paired with the stripped-down business model. But these are unfamiliar and tough environments in which to operate. The frontlines are isolated, far from urban centers, and sit on the edge between stability and chaos. Although these areas are ripe with undeveloped potential, how can businesses manage these new and different risks? Business leaders may seek to mitigate them by adopting a "fast follower" strategy, watching competitors enter early and then learning from their experiences. This would be a mistake, as first movers accrue more than their fair share of advantages in the frontlines. The next chapter discusses the multitude of unfamiliar risks associated with conducting business in the frontlines and the ways to mitigate them to enable you to be the first mover, securing long-term advantages for your business in the process.

CHAPTER 4

Partnerships Mitigate Risk

Leveraging the skills, relationships, and assets of local actors enables business to address the operational challenges inherent in frontline environments, and thereby gain the competitive first-mover advantage.

Continental Gold, a multinational mining corporation from Canada known for its willingness to explore faraway places, struck literal gold in the Andean province of Antioquia in Colombia. The discovery of two rich veins of gold and other minerals in these mountains quickly received an official designation as a Project of National Strategic Interest from the government in Bogota. Large drills, earth movers, and excavation equipment quickly began to appear in the small town of Buritica. However, the large corporation was not the only one racing to make the most of this discovery. Recently erected camps of small-scale, illegal gold miners began to litter the landscape. This was bad news for both Continental Gold and the locals. "Our land has already suffered so much," said Carlos, a proud third-generation coffee grower who had spent his life working on the hillsides of his native province. Although illegal mining operations can be lucrative, they are also incredibly destructive to the environment. Left unregulated, these miners use arsenic to leach gold from the ore, which contaminates the aquifers that provide water to local coffee crops and households. Armed illegal miners also threatened the Canadian geologists and surveyors with violence in an attempt to protect their turf. In a region with a long history of conflict between the government, leftist guerillas, and drug cartels, would this be another instance of competing interests violently creating turmoil and destruction in Antioquia?

Fortunately, Continental Gold's approach to market entry was similar to that of Newmont Mining. Its senior executives were committed not only to mitigating the potential detrimental effects of mining but also to improving the lives of the surrounding communities. Through a series of conversations in Bogota and Medellin, they built nascent relationships with the prominent Federacion Nacional de Cafeteros de Colombia (National Federation of Coffee Growers of Colombia) and one of the country's leading peace-building nongovernmental organizations. After a year of painstaking negotiations, with agreement on multiple addendums outlining their activities, roles, and responsibilities, the three partners collectively launched and cofunded a three-year alliance. This initiative was dedicated to two objectives. First, it sought to increase the economic opportunities and livelihoods of farmers residing in the shadow of the new mine. Second, it launched community-level security measures to improve citizen safety in the area. Each of the partners had its own reasons for the collaboration. The Colombian Coffee Growers Federation was motivated by the possibility of promoting Antioquia as a major coffee-producing region.

Continental Gold was motivated by the prospect of increased stability to develop its mining operations more efficiently. The peace-building NGO was motivated to contribute its long-standing policy expertise in conflict transformation and governance to an area that had been plagued for years by violence.

High-profile initiatives among governments, NGOs, and mining companies do not always produce benefits that trickle down to the local communities. Rather, they live out their impact in shareholder reports and sustainability indices. But this was not the case in Antioquia. This alliance started by serving four hundred families living in the municipalities of Buritica, Cañasgordas, Santa Fe de Antioquia, and Giraldo, delivering economic initiatives such as bringing in experts to train farmers on improved agricultural techniques and providing them with access to small amounts of credit from a revolving fund. Carlos was among the first to sign up for these programs. He learned new ways to improve yields and bean quality on his family's coffee farm. He did not have to worry about finding buyers for his harvest, as the Colombian Coffee Growers Federation arranged for the extra coffee to be absorbed into its own national and international sales efforts. He also enjoyed the spillover economic effects of Continental Gold purchasing most of its supplies locally, further bolstering the regional economy.

The alliance also needed to reshape the security of the region. In Buritica, traditional security measures, such as strengthening the rule of law through enhanced military or police presence, could do more harm than good. The community harbored a deep and largely justified mistrust of local authorities, as the narco-trafficking power in the region, the Clan del Golfo, was rumored to have corrupted local institutions.[1] Instead, the alliance engaged in community-based policing. They organized well-attended training workshops on security and launched community watch groups led by the Guardia Campesina. This largely female informal security organization, with its distinctive bright blue uniforms, is recognized and respected across the country for its independence and protection of human rights in rural territories such as Buritica.

Gradually, these dual economic and security efforts began to pay off. Continental Gold further bolstered the momentum by hiring as many workers locally as possible, thereby increasing incomes in the valley. Carlos watched how some of his neighbors, who had been engaging in illegal mining activities to supplement their family's income, slowly and cautiously turned more of their efforts toward legal farming, given the greater opportunities.

Continental Gold has learned how to mitigate both the competitive and the operational risks associated with frontline environments. Their willingness to invest in tough places like Antioquia, where they are the first large-scale operation, closes off the risk that their competitors will beat them to the opportunity. However, getting there first is not enough. They have also embraced a partner-centered approach that allows them to mitigate the operational risks of the unfamiliar environment. Continental Gold's Buritica mine not only represents Colombia's largest deposit of gold but also boasts the lowest costs of extraction.

Risks of Entry Versus Risks of Not Entering

The risks associated with unfamiliar, ever-changing, and often unstable frontlines would make many business leaders pause. Yet the lesson from the experience of Continental Gold is that those who enter do not have to address the multiple challenges associated with operating in these tough places alone. A whole set of actors is already working in these areas.

With outreach and effort, early introductory discussions can turn into effective partnerships that leverage local skills, relationships, and assets toward common objectives. In Antioquia, Continental Gold's success was due partly to their ability to develop an alliance with prominent and powerful actors. Continental Gold not only contributed $2 million to the overall effort but also invested more than a year building the relationships required to govern the alliance. Together they were able to develop initiatives that not only allowed Continental Gold to safeguard its personnel, property, and operations but also simultaneously to improve the safety and security of those living around the new mine. Continental Gold's financial investment represented a relatively small amount, given the overall capital expenditures to prepare the mine totaled more than $500 million even before the first gold ounce was poured.

Most large companies have already exhausted the easy opportunities for global expansion, and continued growth requires moving into new geographies and markets. Frontline environments represent the future of business growth, and ignoring them puts your business at risk. In fact, the greater risk may be in not investing in such new opportunities and permitting your competitors to move in before you. The underdeveloped conditions of the frontlines hurt the "fast follower" who observes the experience of its competitors. These opportunities are such that the first mover frequently earns disproportionate returns.

Being the first mover is rarely for the faint of heart. That was certainly true during Continental Gold's expansion into Colombia. The government and the former leftist rebels Fuerzas Armadas Revolucionarias de Colombia (Revolutionary Armed Forces of Colombia, or FARC) had just signed their Peace Accords in Havana, formally ending the more than fifty-year-long civil war to great fanfare. Yet within a few months, a slim majority of Colombian voters rejected the peace deal in a referendum, forcing the government and the former rebels back to the negotiating table to pound out modifications to the Peace Accords that Colombian society could accept. Many multinational corporations, including mining companies, decided to delay their foreign direct investments until the political uncertainty subsided.

Nonetheless, Continental Gold pressed on with its investments. And it paid off. After significant upfront capital expenditures, its Buritica mine has, with its annual gold production of 265,000 ounces and 4.7 million ounces of reserves, essentially doubled the country's entire gold production. In the following five years, fellow multinational mining corporations, including BHP Billiton, Anglo-American, Glencore, and Drummond have invested nearly $2 billion in Colombia. And although the competitors have followed quickly, Continental Gold retains the first-mover advantage. Located only ninety minutes away from Colombia's second city, Medellin, along the well paved Pan-American Highway, the Buritica mine required none of the infrastructure investments in roads, power generation, and communication that mining giants usually have to construct to gain access to remote mineral reserves. As a consequence, the mine has the lowest all-in sustaining extraction costs in Colombia, the industry's leading metric of efficient gold production.

Mining and natural resource are not the only industries that can generate such large first-mover advantages in frontline environments. For a number of years, United Airlines both invested in an aircraft maintenance hub in the San Pedro Sula airport in Honduras and worked closely with national and municipal government officials to transform the regulations governing airlines in the country. This effort led to a law promoting low-cost flights into San Pedro Sula, cutting the landing and takeoff tariffs by 75 percent. Fellow international airlines, including American, Delta, JetBlue, Volaris, and Southwest added flights from the

United States to San Pedro Sula: more than one hundred weekly flights today. And incidentally, although plenty of airlines have followed its lead, United still retains that first-mover advantage we've seen among companies willing to invest into frontline markets—30 percent of seats in and out of San Pedro Sula are still controlled by United.

When a Chinese mining company, Zijin, put in an offer of $1.4 billion to purchase Continental Gold at the end of 2019, the company's public statements cited the Buritica mine as the justification both for the acquisition and its valuation.[2] Upon completing the acquisition of Continental Gold, Zijin abruptly discontinued the alliance's three-year economic and security program. Making a deal with the Colombian Coffee Growers Federation and a peace-building NGO appeared as nonessential expenses to the Buritica mine's new Chinese owners.[3] Unfortunately, nefarious elements have since reemerged around Buritica, as have illegal mining operations. Given the recent increase in violence, instability, and competition from illegal miners in Antioquia, Zijin has suffered work stoppages and incurred additional security costs to protect its personnel and property that it had not previously accounted for.[4] Partnerships like those represented in this tripartite alliance can be the difference between success and failure in the frontlines. And as the community has been left again to fend for itself in the deteriorating security situation, Carlos expressed the sentiments widely held across the valley: "We sure wish we could trade the Chinese miners and get back our Canadian friends."

Leveraging Nontraditional Partners to Mitigate Risk

Among the many lessons from Continental Gold's experience with its Buritica mine is that businesses need not and should not navigate all of the associated frontline risks on their own. The frontline operating model depends on controlling those steps where the business possesses a unique competitive advantage and then partnering with local organizations to manage the remaining activities. However, the key success factor rests on building relationships with multiple nontraditional partners to help manage challenges facing operations, many of which business is unaccustomed to dealing with. As such, businesses will encounter the following organizations in the frontlines, each with their own needs, processes, and aspirations: governments; nongovernmental organizations; military and police; insurgents, guerillas, and criminal elements; and the communities themselves.

Governments. Although frontline environments stretch beyond national borders into isolated regions where governments often have little reach, any efforts to work in these environments require some level of engagement with the various levels of government. National governments in developing countries are often fragile, and their primary focus is frequently on achieving unified control over national territory rather than on development outcomes. Even when they prioritize economic and social development initiatives, they often emphasize centrality of governance rather than the needs of rural populations.[5] Those living in frontline environments also face tensions between national and regional or local priorities. In particular, in disputed territories, local governments or other forces may actively oppose or passively subvert national priorities. In these cases, local administration may either be imposed directly by national governments and lack popular support or be taken over by these opposing groups who may or may not prioritize the provision of social services such as health care or education. In either case, business must navigate the complicated coordination of basic security and rule of law with these parties.

Nongovernment Organizations. In most frontline environments, NGOs provide most of the social services that would normally be delivered by governments. Although individual NGOs vary in their specific mission and funding, what unites them is the overall goal of alleviating individual suffering. Many NGOs have been working in frontline environments for decades and, as a result, have deep and meaningful relationships with a variety of stakeholders. Their technical skills, knowledge, and long-term programming commitment develop the necessary foundational infrastructure for a thriving community—things like water, sanitation, health care, and education. Finally, NGOs work closely with one another and have a well-established system for multi-actor coordination. In fact, there is even a specific title, "chief of party," for the individual who is responsible for coordinating the various actors on a given project.

Former secretary of state Hillary Clinton once said, "Aid chases need, while investment chases opportunity."[6] Although NGOs often do great work, their goal isn't explicitly economic growth. They deal with emergencies such as natural disasters or war, where the imperative is to serve as temporary intermediaries to fill voids in essential services until such a time as the state has the capacity to step into its responsibility. Ideally, NGOs should move on once the initial turbulent period has passed. However, new problems tend to emerge more quickly than the capacity of the government or the community to address them, which provides a rationale for NGOs to remain in the area and continue their work.

As donor fatigue sets in even as their mandate continues or expands, NGOs often have innovated in the business space, attempting to build programming that helps their beneficiaries start businesses to bolster their livelihoods. However, without the proper business knowledge, their good intentions can either destabilize a local market or force entrepreneurship on those who have neither the skills nor desire for it.[7] As a result, in many frontline environments, these entrepreneurship programs shift the responsibility of growing local economies from governments and businesses onto the backs of the poor, who must absorb the risk inherent in new ventures.

Nevertheless, with their local knowledge, expertise, and relationships, NGOs can become a critical partner to businesses on their expansion into frontline environments. The common ground that NGOs and businesses frequently share is the creation of economic opportunity. NGOs value increased jobs as a way to sustainably reduce poverty, while business needs NGOs to help manage each step of their value chain to gain access to raw material supply or to produce products customers value and want to buy.

Military/Police. Businesses must also engage with whichever actors control a territory. In some cases, this takes the form of internationally backed troops or peacekeepers, such as foreign armies, the United Nations, or the African Union, who are deployed into frontline territories. When this happens, they likely share a common interest with business in increasing stability and creating economic opportunity. As one US Army General noted to us, "Economic efforts [are] an example of the new roles [that] the U.S. military will have to play outside of traditional armed conflict."[8] The United States is not alone. Canada, the United Kingdom, Australia, and Norway have consciously fostered civilian-military cooperation in post-conflict zones to extend and protect economic initiatives.[9]

In other cases, the country's military or police force or even an informal security organization such as the Guardia Campesina in Colombia may control the territory. Sadly, however, in most of our experience working in frontline environments, local communities do not benefit from the presence of national militaries or police forces, given the high levels of endemic corruption, so they may not be ideal partners for local initiatives. That said, businesses should always meet local representatives of the military and police, at minimum, to share the latest security assessments.

Insurgents, Guerillas, Gangs, Traffickers. In many areas of rural and sometimes contested terrain, security is often left to insurgents, guerillas, and even criminal elements, such as gangs and traffickers, who move into a power vacuum and compete for control.[10] Some try to win the support of the locals through basic services, but more often they exert control through coercion. They employ forced labor, offer below-market pricing, and run corrupt organizations that impersonate legitimate businesses. However, there is no escaping the important role of these actors in the frontlines. At worst, they are competitors to legitimate business with an unfair advantage. At best, a portion of them can be co-opted.

Business must, at minimum, acknowledge who controls the territory. International and local laws prohibit working directly with criminal elements. Even if the chances of being caught are low, it is our position that the reputational risk is prohibitive. What we have found working in impoverished, lawless regions, however, is that sometimes those involved in nefarious activities are looking for legitimate employment and can provide insight on how to navigate these challenges. At other times, even seemingly reputable actors hide their vested interests. Thus, being savvy about where the power lies is essential.

Local Communities. The most critical players in frontline environments are members of the community itself. Village elders, leaders of Indigenous communities, or religious figures often have disproportionate informal power and influence, as they provide governance, adjudicate small disagreements, and serve as gatekeepers to communities.

Our first stop upon arriving in a new community is always to meet with both the formal and the informal local leaders to ask permission to engage with their people. Many frontline communities may be initially skeptical of outsiders, because their experience most likely entails foreigners arriving, promising much, delivering little, and then exiting, never to be seen again. Nevertheless, business needs frontline communities for their knowledge, labor, and access to resources. What unites communities is their desire for a chance at a better life for their children, for which a steady job in a viable enterprise is a tremendous first step. And thus, at the most basic level, business and local communities share tremendous potential common ground.

Mapping the Landscape of Actors in the Frontlines

Given the importance of developing partnerships, how can businesses start the process of cultivating ties with local actors that will best help them to explore the context and work effectively on the ground? Forming these partnerships becomes critical to de-risking a new venture, as a diverse array of allies will maximize information, networks, and resources available for your work in the frontlines. First and foremost, we suggest that partnerships be thought of as ends in themselves rather than means to an end. If these relationships are merely symbolic, to signal legitimacy, they will likely only provide superficial insights. Rather, effective partnerships are those where both sides seek out the other's counsel, recognize each other's strengths, and share common objectives. Second, effective partnerships evolve over time. We are often wary of those who are quick to jump at the chance to collaborate without taking the time to understand our values and approach. Rather, we appreciate partners who ask as many questions of us as we do of them. It is notable that it took

Continental Gold almost a year to negotiate the terms of the three-way alliance in Antioquia. Testing the waters of collaboration before diving in remains essential, as your first foray into the frontlines will rarely yield the most potent collaborations. However, it will start conversations that may later blossom into mutually beneficial relationships.

One of our partners, a Filipino peace-building organization, does this particularly well, as exemplified by the way they cautiously launched programs in the southern island of Mindanao. The conflict in the region has lasted five centuries and continues to the present.[11] The Muslim population, the Moros, who claim never to have succumbed to Spanish colonial rule, protest that the dominant Filipino Catholic national identity leaves no room for the unique expression of their religion and heritage. More recently, in 1972, the Moro National Liberation Front was launched to fulfill the aspirations of the Moro community but quickly splintered into rival guerrilla factions, some fighting for Moro self-rule, and others fighting to create an Islamic state in the Philippines. From this turmoil, the Moro Islamic Liberation Front emerged as the strongest force. After decades of conflict, the Filipino government and Moro leaders finally negotiated and signed a comprehensive peace agreement in 2014. In return for thousands of Moro insurgents demobilizing, the Manila government promised that the Philippine Congress would approve the law creating a new Muslim autonomous region called Bangsamoro.[12]

The signing of the comprehensive peace agreement catalyzed new economic and social initiatives in the formerly inaccessible territory of Mindanao, with our Filipino NGO partner leading the efforts. As a peace-building NGO focused on reincorporating demobilized fighters back into rural villages, it is particularly attuned to listening to people from all sides of the decades-long insurgency. Their staff has a deep understanding how Mindanao's massive socioeconomic disparities, with less than one-tenth of the income per person as the rest of the Philippines, reinforce its religious and ethnic ones.[13] Before they begin to work in any community—Moro Muslim, Filipino Catholic, or ethnic Lumad—the staff talks to as many potential stakeholders as possible to ensure that it is getting a variety of perspectives on the challenges facing these communities. For example, had this NGO listened only to the elites in Manila about the security situation in the provinces of Maguindanao, Lanao del Sur, and Lanao del Norte, they would have never considered working there. A UNICEF director told us, "No one goes to this part of Mindanao, not even us. With remnants of dissident Moro insurgents, Islamic extremists, Abu Sayaff, and marauding drug gangs, it is just too dangerous."

Before beginning their inclusive rural development projects in the new self-governing Muslim region, the NGO team spent well over a week driving more than a thousand kilometers around the entire territory from Cagayan de Oro in the north to Cotabato in the south to meet local Muslim imams, Catholic priests and bishops, community elders, farming cooperative managers, illegal miners, businessmen, the staff of other NGOs, dissidents, mayors, and the governor. This allowed them to effectively characterize the actors in the territory, better understand the various communities' needs, and discover potentially useful and underutilized resources. This broad research can be time consuming, arduous, and expensive. But it is indispensable because it avoids a single perspective dominating any decision. Such an investment of time and resources ensures that the NGO's efforts are not inadvertently co-opted by actors looking to serve their own interests. It also gives its staff insight into the simmering issues and potentially conflicting perspectives that could later pose a risk to their personnel and programs in the region.

What the Filipino peace-building NGO calls "mapping the landscape" many qualitative researchers call "purposeful sampling." Rather than looking for an average case, it involves looking for the maximum amount of variation and even extreme cases to understand unusual situations. This approach differs from "opportunistic sampling," which involves gathering information from whomever you encounter, or snowball methods, where one contact can connect you to others, both of which are easier to implement but likely to generate more narrow and biased information.[14] We suggest that selecting partners for entry into frontline environments should follow the same underlying principles. Rather than choosing partners based on ease, look for a variety of potential partners to maximize breadth of information. Intentionally seek out different perspectives. Pay particular attention to spanning generational, geographical, socioeconomic, ethnic, and religious divides. Consider the variety of circumstances that you might encounter and the different things you might need under those circumstances. For example, how might this partner fare under a different political regime or in an emergency? How would these situations shape the information that you might receive?

We acknowledge that the task of mapping the multitude of local actors in a new territory takes time and effort and forces you to go beyond the comfort of close connections. This is not an efficient process. It requires building relationships in unlikely places. It may also cause discomfort among existing local partners who want to shape your experiences to match their own perspectives and interests. But in the end, the benefits of working with unusual frontline partners are well worth the effort in cultivating these ties. Investments in early relationship building, which are most often investments of time, can help ensure that more significant subsequent investments of capital are directed in the most effective way. They provide new and valuable perspectives and improve the quality of information used to make decisions, particularly in regions where a business's past successes in other parts of the world may not directly translate.

An African proverb captures the challenges posed by a firm's reticence to invest in frontline environments: "The best time to plant a new tree is twenty years ago. The second best time is now."[15] The task may seem daunting. You may wish that you had started to build the foundation much earlier and lament the long time it may take to yield results. However, further delay will not speed up the process. Delay only serves to limit your access to the sunlight as others grow around you.

In Part I of this book, we have established the business case for investment in frontline environments. Although traditional business wisdom might have suggested steering clear of these unfamiliar and uncertain regions, we have shown that investments in frontline environments can actually reduce costs, mitigate risk, and unlock valuable new sources of supplies. Companies, particularly those in economic sectors that take advantage of underdeveloped land and inefficiencies in labor and capital such as agriculture, infrastructure, and mining, are likely to lead the way. But as businesses build operations and hire local employees, this increased local income will provide the next round of investment opportunities for companies in other sectors such as financial services, telecommunications, retail, and consumer goods. The first movers will earn the rewards.

However, entry into these environments will inevitably expose businesses to a vast array of new challenges. To grow and profit in these tough parts of the world, business will require a new set of tools. Part II addresses these challenges by outlining the essential elements of the process that turns frontline business opportunities into a reality.

The Process

CHAPTER 5

Follow the Money

Identify economic opportunities by following the money across the
value chain from beginning to end in an industry and a geography.

On both of our desks, amid photos of our loved ones, sits a framed image of a circle of feet adorned with a variety of footwear, from flip flops to heels. These feet belong to fourteen survivors of child sex trafficking whom we met in a safe house in the Philippines. We were there in 2016 at the invitation of World Vision, a Christian child-focused humanitarian organization, to help them extend their work to combat the trafficking of children into the sex trade. We keep the photo on our desks to remind us of both the resilient spirit of those girls and the value that business perspectives can have in changing lives. Indeed, following their footsteps on the terrible journey they had taken from their villages to eventual safety reflects the heart of the Business on the Frontlines process—which always begins by following the money.

Every year, more than twenty million people around the world are caught in the web of human trafficking. Well over half are forced into the sex industry through fraud or coercion, nearly a quarter of them children.[1] The Philippines, in particular, is a global hot spot for child sex trafficking—UNICEF estimates between sixty thousand and a hundred thousand children are trafficked there annually.[2] Like in other remittance-based economies, many poor Filipinos from the countryside travel elsewhere for work. It can be nearly impossible for a family to recognize a trafficker posing as a recruiter for legitimate domestic work who will then entrap and force their child into the brothels in Manila or on tourist islands.

This project represented a significant departure from the agriculture- and resource-based market creation initiatives on which we had built our reputation for success. Although we are used to interacting with unsavory actors, thinking of human trafficking as a business problem raised eyebrows even among those who knew our work well. In fact, we were unsure how we might respond when coming face to face with the modern slavery happening every day around the world. However, we believed that looking at this devastating problem through the lens of business principles and processes might add a new perspective and generate the seeds of innovative interventions. Fortunately, we found an equally forward-looking partner in World Vision Philippines and its national director then, Josaias "Jody" Dela Cruz.

With his youthful energy, a penchant for Jollibee burgers, and lovely tenor voice singing at the karaoke bar, Jody's cheerful and welcoming manner belied his more than twenty years of deep, committed service to those children forgotten and abandoned by Filipino society. Whether it be to find homes for street children or reduce dangerous child labor practices, Jody prioritized World Vision programs that would help the most vulnerable children live their lives to the fullest. World Vision, the largest nonprofit in the Philippines has been serving there since 1955, with programs supporting 1.5 million children every year.[3]

As part of our predeparture preparation, and with the help from the team at World Vision, we surveyed the multiple existing programs across Filipino NGOs designed to fight sex trafficking. It became immediately apparent that these programs focused almost exclusively on prevention or rehabilitation. Prevention efforts consisted primarily of social media campaigns aimed at increasing public awareness of the tactics of recruiters. Rehabilitation programs helped survivors find safe homes, work, and a new life for victims lucky enough to escape. However, there were no interventions focused on anything that happened between the initial recruitment and the rare rescue, and as a result, our understanding of what happened to trafficking victims during this time was a black box. This was notable from a business perspective, as the value chain through which an organization goes from "acquisition of raw materials" to "sales of end products" is often complex and vulnerable. Of course, we do not perceive children as products or commodities. But sex trafficking, as horrific as it is, is a business, and the criminal syndicates engaging in it certainly see children that way. Our process suggests that using value chain analysis and mapping the revenues and costs at each step is at the heart of our ability to examine any economic system. In this case, our objective was to disrupt it.

We investigated part of the revenue side of the value chain from our US living rooms, as international tourists are an important customer segment in the Filipino sex industry. Posing as potential clients, we approached travel agencies inquiring about different options for sex holidays. One afternoon, two men in gray suits unexpectedly showed up on the doorstep of one of our students' apartments. After a number of frantic phone calls, our team sat down to explain the purpose of our research with what turned out to be two FBI agents sent to investigate the red flags triggered by our extensive activity on the dark web. Despite being flagged by the authorities, these exploratory efforts were invaluable, as they provided us with a baseline for the revenue associated with child prostitution. Moreover, even businesses with good intentions must be mindful of inadvertently crossing the line into legal jeopardy as they explore frontline opportunities.

Once in the Philippines, our team checked these revenue estimates by inquiring at massage parlors and brothels, some of which were hidden in plain sight in ordinary-looking shopping malls and others we found in dark corners of the red light districts in Manila and on the island of Cebu. We talked to everyone who might give us their perspective, including clients, prostitutes, pimps, madams, and hotel concierges. We even interviewed a number of off-duty police officers working second jobs as security for the brothels. We learned that the price for a trafficked child was about $20 per hour and $60–$100 per night, based on the types of sex acts and the age of the child. Occasionally, the police would barge in and arrest the children, but they have a great deal of incentive to look the other way for a bribe of about $300.

On the supply side, we traced the journey of a trafficked young person from beginning to end, noting the costs and risks for traffickers at each step. This involved more than eighty interviews with social workers, health officials, lawyers, prosecutors, government officials, anti-trafficking and humanitarian NGOs, doctors, and staff from the International Justice Mission and the International Labor Organization. Next, we conducted focus groups with survivors in safe homes, all of which helped our team draw a detailed picture of how the industry works.

The value chain breaks down this way: Recruiters, often women who were previously trafficked themselves, go to remote villages to procure children, especially young girls, by offering families $30 per child with the promise of remittances. Even though they know trusting a recruiter is risky, the lack of meaningful opportunities leaves many impoverished girls and their families willing to take the risk for a better life for the whole family. The recruiters are paid $50 per child. Groups of three to five children are moved by bus or ferry to Manila, Cebu, or other large prostitution centers. Travel costs for the group are approximately $200, the largest expense being bribes for not having the paperwork required for travel within the Philippines. Thus, the upfront, one-time investment for recruitment and transportation is about $150 per child.

Once a child reaches their destination, a new set of costs emerge associated with holding children at a brothel. They include the expected line items of housing, food, hygiene, and clothing, as well as a supply of illegal drugs, as addiction makes it easier to control trafficked children. These costs total to between $700 and $800 per year. Additional operational costs, like the cut of the profits that goes to pimps, the salaries for security guards, and bribes to local police amount to an additional $2,000 per year.

Let us pause and reflect on the tragedy here. These are innocent victims. Mostly young women already facing poverty. Often relying on the kindness of strangers and a hope for a better life, they are ensnared, imprisoned, and treated like disposable commodities. The horror really hit home while listening to the youngest victim in a safe house who, at the time, was the same age as Viva's daughter, Ava—nine.

Human traffickers can earn between US$3,000 and US$10,000 a year on a trafficked child, between 20 percent and over three times more than the average per capita GDP in the Philippines.[4] With acquisition costs under $200 and annual operational costs at about $2,800, there is the potential for thousands of dollars of profit a year, all of which goes into the pockets of criminals.

However, once we understood the value chain, we could identify its weak points. By asking questions and listening to the diversity of voices and stories we were gathering, to our surprise, the weakest link appeared to be the pimps—the (mostly) men who worked in red light districts negotiating with customers and bribing police. As we interviewed them, inquiring about their lives without judgment, we learned that many worked second jobs to earn enough to pay for necessities and school fees for their own children. Most were in debt to more powerful criminals, mainly because of drug addiction or gambling, and were stuck in a never-ending cycle of debt. Our proposal was to focus on enticing them away from their current positions by connecting them with jobs in the shipping, fishing, and booming construction industry.

When we presented our suggestions to World Vision staff, silence descended upon the meeting room. Many initially balked at the idea of developing programming that would assist pimps to find alternative employment. World Vision staff see themselves as a child-focused advocacy and humanitarian organization and couldn't fathom rewarding those who had exploited children with well-paying jobs. But after their initial shock wore off, Jody not only led a disciplined process in which the staff weighed the various ethical and moral issues but also ultimately concluded, "Let's try it." Based on his brave leadership, World Vision decided that programs to redirect pimps were a pragmatic approach to undermining the system of traffickers. Staff members reached out to their contacts at maritime and construction companies, and together they designed programs to hire former pimps into fishing and building trades.

We are not suggesting that we found a solution to the global challenge of sex trafficking. Any long-term, comprehensive solution will require a multipronged effort including enforcing existing anti-trafficking laws, economic development in impoverished rural areas, and cultural change that values women and girls. Further, any gains are likely to be only temporary, as there are many actors waiting in the wings to take the place of the pimps that World Vision successfully draws into legitimate employment. However, from the perspective of our partner, any opportunity to disrupt a value chain in a particular location is useful as it slows down an operation, thereby creating a window for other interventions to prevent recruitment and rescue enslaved children.

This initiative clearly demonstrates that incorporating business principles can contribute novel insights to some of the world's toughest problems that have long been the purview of humanitarian organizations and governments. Our intention is not to transform NGOs into market actors or to imply that humanitarian problems are only business problems. However, by increasing the diversity of people working on a problem and including their perspectives into the conversation, new and innovative solutions can emerge to address entrenched challenges.

This approach works best when combined with the vast expertise of the professionals already working on the issue. Research on diversity has routinely demonstrated that bringing together people of different national backgrounds and functional perspectives results in improved creativity.[5] In the Philippines, we didn't just bring together a business perspective with that of our NGO partner; we also elevated the often ignored voices of the pimps, prostitutes, and police officers who constituted and participated in the system of trafficking. It was only through considering the diversity of their experiences and interests that we were able to reframe the problem in a way that none of us could have done alone.

However, the mere presence of diverse perspectives is not enough to generate innovation. Our work with World Vision would not have been possible if we had not invested in building an effective work process that integrated our skills with our partners' existing capabilities. Leaning on their strategic flexibility and deep situational expertise not only facilitated the generation of ideas but also fostered our partner's willingness to act upon them.[6] By working closely together and leveraging our diverse strengths, we reshaped how World Vision combats trafficking in the Philippines. Further, effectively applying our "follow-the-money" process to this heinous criminal operation reaffirmed our confidence in our approach. Indeed, business principles and tools can become invaluable in helping to solve some of the world's toughest problems.

Guidelines to Follow the Money to Map Value Chains in the Frontlines

Although most frontline opportunities focus on sectors such as agriculture, infrastructure, mining, consumer goods, and manufacturing, we chose to describe our process with an example from the child sex trafficking industry. Criminal elements run this value chain like a business, no matter how repulsive. We use this case to show that through diligent effort, combined with pragmatic data gathering and economic logic, almost any value chain of any industry in any geography can be mapped. This analytical exercise represents the first step in assessing potential opportunities in the frontlines, as the detailed understanding of the economics of any industry is a nonnegotiable precondition to subsequent idea generation, business case development, rapid idea testing, and ultimately investment and expansion. Furthermore, the process of following the money, although first explained through value chain analysis, can then be applied across an entire economic system in a territory to unearth further opportunities.

Begin by drawing a basic diagram of each step that a product takes from raw material inputs to sales to a customer. This value chain begins with the supply chains that acquire raw materials and then extends to include all business activities that support the design and sale of products to customers. To illustrate, for agriculture, the steps include land, seeds, labor, sowing, fertilizer and pesticides, harvest, transportation, processing, storage, further transportation, wholesale, retail, and end customer. For mineral extraction, the steps include land, licenses, geology, discovery, infrastructure such as roads, communications, training for skilled workers, equipment, excavation, metallurgy, transportation, shipping, wholesale, retail, and end customer. Economic logic dictates that if for-profit enterprises operate in an industry in a geography, they have a way to make a profit and earn returns on investment. In general, then, the expenses associated with inputs combined with the costs of each incremental step in the value chain must be below the ultimate price the customer pays for the product.

Moving from the theoretical to the practical, you need to take this basic diagram of the value chain and conduct multiple interviews with various actors at each step to determine the costs and prices. Starting at both ends of the value chain and moving toward the center brings structure to this ambitious but highly ambiguous problem-solving approach. For example, if exploring the agricultural sector, some teammates should start at the beginning of the value chain and try to buy seeds or seedlings, while other teammates focus on the other end by shopping for produce in local markets. Transportation to those local markets, access to credit, processing, storage, and other business activities need to be calculated as well. It is important to factor in the quality standards required for international exports, which are frequently difficult to achieve in nascent frontline markets. As such, it's useful to focus on domestic markets first and then expand from there. Further, pay attention to units. Not a small number of our teams have been tripped up in mapping value chains by mixing up units of analysis such as yields per hectare versus acre, price per kilogram versus ounce, and time measured in months, harvests, or years.

The sheer lack of data and level of uncertainty in frontline environments demands triangulation of critical information across multiple data sources, until such time as the information from each incremental interview harmonizes with the data gained from previous interviews.[7] The farmers, fishermen, and other producers in poor remote areas are often incredible sources of vital information. However, other actors in the frontlines frequently possess a chokehold on some critical aspect of the value chain, such as market information, transportation, storage, communication, or access to credit. For example, in Chapter 1 the armed middlemen in Western Uganda had a monopoly on transportation across the long distance to Kampala, the capital. Such actors then use this market power to exploit the situation and capture more money for themselves. These actors may be less directly forthcoming about the economics of their arrangements. You will know when it is time to transition from intensive data collection to intensive analysis once information-gathering activity hits diminishing returns on gaining incremental insights.

Following the money through an entire value chain can help uncover the obstacles to further economic activity. While working in the Amazon on the pirarucu supply chain, as described in Chapter 3, our team quickly figured out the price per kilogram of pirarucu that the middlemen paid at the dock deep in the Amazon versus the prices paid by fish processors a thousand miles downriver in Manaus. We also determined the prices paid by Brazilian families in supermarkets over time, with the prices spiking over Holy Week, a full four months after the pirarucu fishing season ended. Yet the purchase of boats would show a payback in a reasonable timeframe only if first, we could buy them at a decent price, and second, these boats had refrigerated holds and engines with reasonable diesel efficiency. With our local partners, our team marched down to the docks in Manaus to investigate the boat resale market. We found boats for sale at our price point with diesel engines that would work, but not the eight we needed. We then trooped over to the only two shipwrights in Manaus to determine the cost and timing of ordering new boats, because the river communities needed them by August, when the pirarucu season started. With the patient support of our local partner each step of the way, the river communities purchased the boats in time for most of them to be delivered before the start of the fishing season.

Evaluating new opportunities in the frontlines requires following the money as a first step. This mindset can and should be applied not only to an industry value chain but also to an entire economic system within a territory. We illustrate this approach with the following example from Bosnia.

Determining Needed Economic Activity in Bosnia

We stood in a rocky field on the outskirts of Srebrenica, staring at a shell of a utilitarian-looking structure that was to become apartments for refugees. Srebrenica is known for the July 1995 massacre by Bosnian Serb forces of more than eight thousand Bosnian Muslim boys and men and the expulsion of more than twenty thousand civilians from the city, in what came to be known as ethnic cleansing. We were accompanied by our partner, Catholic Relief Services (CRS), who was in charge of this initiative, and Jusuf, a former businessman and now assistant to the mayor of the city. This complex, located close to the site where so many Muslim boys and men were murdered, was going to be transformed into a lively symbol of Srebrenica's resurrection.

CRS came to Bosnia in 1993 to provide emergency relief to the Bosnian people living under the siege of Sarajevo by Serb forces during the Balkan Wars (1992–1995). Their staff earned the respect and affection of the Bosnian people because they were one of the few international NGOs that remained during the 1,425-day siege, the longest in the history of modern warfare. Indeed, at great risk to themselves, CRS staff smuggled in badly needed items, such as baby formula, through hidden supply tunnels. This wartime service made CRS a trusted partner for peace building after the conflict. In addition to developing social programs that addressed trauma and encouraged tolerance and forgiveness, they also assisted in repatriating the more than four million people displaced by the war—half the country's population—by either returning them to their homes or finding them new housing. Almost eight thousand people, mostly widows, children, and those injured during the war, still lingered in refugee camps fifteen years after the war ended.

As we walked around the grim structure, with the bitter January wind shearing across the open landscape, Jusuf, a short, stocky man well into his fifties, relayed his vision for the place. Jusuf's family had experienced tragic losses during the Balkan Wars but he was nonetheless excited about the social housing construction project and imagined a future for this community with a school nearby. However, we were immediately skeptical of the complete absence of any signs of modern life amid the concrete and steel. We were miles from the nearest market. There was no traffic passing by. It seemed like a forgotten, isolated place.

These apartments were designed as low-cost housing for returning refugees, but the residents would still need to pay their rent and utilities, buy food, and address their daily needs. The international charity that had sustained them in the refugee camps would not last forever. The residents of these apartments still had to have jobs to earn the income needed to pay their bills. One of our students spoke the words on all our minds: "But what are they going to do out here?" Jusuf stopped talking, and after a long pause, his proud expression melted away. We stood in silence.

It was clear that all parties had the best of intentions. It had taken years to find the land and secure international donor funding for the construction. The apartments would have heat and water and provide safety for those who had been left behind and lost the most during the war. However, the government officials, the NGOs and the donors had been so busy figuring out how to resettle these refugees, they forgot to consider what would happen once these immediate needs were met. It was clear that our common challenge was to make the apartment complex into both the vibrant economy and community that Jusuf imagined. On the current path, however, his vision was not an inevitable outcome.

We remained silent during the long drive across the snowy mountains back to CRS's offices in Sarajevo, but the moment we settled into a small conference room, we burst into action, furiously debriefing our observations on whiteboards and covering the table with the building's architectural plans. We knew that many of the refugees were educated and skilled. Bosnian society prizes education for men and women. However, there were few jobs available in the country, and even fewer of them nearby. Even if they were close by, most large companies prioritized hiring returning combatants, not refugees. No outside economic force or other businesses would be coming to their rescue. The returning refugees would need to create their own economic opportunities right where they were going to live. We needed to create the conditions to jump-start this new community's economic recovery.

Looking at the building plans, we saw that if we turned the ground floor of the building into an inviting commercial space and rerouted local traffic, we could entice other Bosnians to locate their business there. We could also reserve some of the space for the returning refugees to start their own ventures. Once we got through all of the steps of translation, Jusuf loved the suggestion. The local government and CRS also embraced the idea. Luckily, construction had only just begun, and it was possible to modify the architectural plans. CRS agreed to offer coaching support for entrepreneurs. In the end, this building became home to several hundred refugees, and the ground floor became home to small businesses, including hairdressers, grocers, mechanics, and carpentry shops. CRS replicated these plans in the six other cities in Bosnia where they were building social housing. The project quickly scaled past the first seven CRS-sponsored housing complexes. Bosnia's national government adopted it as official policy for refugee housing. Since 2015, almost 3,200 of these social housing units have been built, a quarter which have ground floors dedicated to businesses, yielding hundreds of buzzing start-ups and thousands of new employment opportunities to assist the communities to build resilience and stability themselves.[8]

The basic profit motive that drives actors across a value chain in an industry or the economy of a territory should not be feared. Market transactions for labor or goods and services when at an equilibrium are voluntary and can and do enrich the lives of both buyers and sellers. Competition at each step checks excessive self-interest and value capture. However, what needs to be safeguarded against is control of a choke point along the value chain by a single monopolist or cartel. If they dominate critical factors such as information or transportation or access to credit, then oligopolists can abuse their power and exploit the powerless.

Following the money and embracing market discipline is the pragmatic first step in evaluating potential frontline opportunities. Launching early data-gathering interviews to delineate expansion options will quickly and inevitably lead to a myriad of local actors presenting themselves as potential partners for the venture. Yet in such unfamiliar circumstances, how should businesses determine which among the countless actors to trust? The next chapter presents the strategy of partnering broadly to gather the information needed to make informed business decisions.

CHAPTER 6

Partner Broadly

*Find the right partners and take time to develop the relationships
needed to gather information that benefits all parties and safeguards
investment.*

For thirty-four days in 2006, the blue sky of Beirut was darkened
with thick black smoke as an estimated 170,000 shells fell from the
sky and turned neighborhoods into rubble.[1] Known as the July War
in Lebanon and the Second Lebanon War in Israel, the conflict began
when Hezbollah, the part militia / part political party that governs
most of Lebanon's southern region and the eastern Bekaa Valley, kidnapped two Israeli soldiers. Hezbollah, which builds up popular support through its vast network of social services, is committed to the
destruction of Israel.[2] As a result of Hezbollah's targeted campaign
against Israel, the 2006 conflict killed more than one thousand and displaced almost one million Lebanese civilians.[3]

In 2009, three years after the war ended, we walked through the rubble of the Dahiyah suburb of Beirut. We met our host for the day, a local businessman named Khalil, through our partner, a large international NGO. Importing and exporting is the lifeblood of the Lebanese economy, making up almost 70 percent of its economic activity.[4] Starting out as a simple merchant and trader, Khalil had turned his import and export business in electronics and commercial goods into an empire by Lebanese standards. He was about forty-five years old, weathered in appearance but jovial in demeanor. During the weeks and months after the ceasefire, Khalil had served as a lifeline to those whose lives had been turned upside down, coordinating with humanitarian organizations to facilitate search and rescue, emergency assistance, and rebuilding efforts. He seemed to know everyone in the neighborhood by name. Throughout our day together, our discussions were punctuated by dozens of small interruptions by locals approaching Khalil, each of which felt like a continuation of conversations that had begun earlier. Khalil would handle the matter and then turn back to our team:

"Her son has been getting into some trouble lately, and she wanted me to speak with him."

"His daughter is getting married next month."

"Her husband is looking for a job."

"They are looking to replace some chairs at the school and I connected them with a friend."

He supplied these matter-of-fact explanations after each interruption, providing context to the back-and-forth that sometimes switched between English, French, and Arabic. It seemed that, even in one of the most densely populated cities in one of the most densely populated countries in the world, nothing got done without involving Khalil. When we returned two years later, we found the neighborhood was largely rebuilt.[5] Khalil was still there, running his electronics import/export business, solving problems, attending weddings and funerals, and finding jobs for the unemployed.

On a subsequent visit to Lebanon a few years later, we sat with Naji in the beautiful seaside neighborhood of Raouché in a Beirut cafe overlooking the famous Corniche rock as the sun set over the Mediterranean. Some of the world's best chickpeas grow just forty miles from the city in the central Bekaa Valley, which is famous for its microclimates and fertile soil. Naji, an entrepreneur with investments in software development, venture capital, a start-up accelerator, and even a vineyard, had spent the day with us, traipsing through the fields, eagerly pointing out the different chickpea varieties that grew between small leaves. Naji was just as at home in those fields as he was in this upscale restaurant, where he often entertained guests in his role on the Board of Directors of Cortas, the country's largest and oldest food processor.

We met Naji through the University of Notre Dame network. He was a proud graduate of the Class of 1987. Like Khalil, Naji sported salt-and-pepper hair, and his weathered features frequently broke into a quick smile. As we shared a bottle of Lebanese red wine, Naji described the day-to-day challenges of the chickpea farmers as if they were his own. He worried about Lebanon's ability to absorb the influx of Syrian refugees, lamenting the war in "his neighborhood." Farmers pitched tents on their fields to house the Syrian families and then Naji deployed his vast business and social network to connect the newcomers with schools, jobs, and other support. As he spoke, we wondered how he had time for his commercial ventures given that helping to resettle thousands of Syrians appeared to be a full-time job.

Both Kahlil and Naji seemed like they would be useful partners to help us navigate the Lebanese commercial landscape. But how did we know whom to trust? This is a key question when working in frontline environments, and it's not always an easy one to answer. As it turned out, it was almost impossible to know that one of these two men shouldn't be trusted. We wager that no outsider would reasonably be able to predict that collaborating with one of them would be a violation of US federal law.[6] The challenge of whom to trust was amplified in this case because of the striking similarities between them, both in appearance and manner. They were both warm and welcoming, competent and confident. Both were exceptionally well connected. Trusted partners vouched for both of them. They both had entrepreneurial backgrounds, having built successful businesses from the ground up. Both spoke passionately about their love of their country and their desire to create opportunities for the most vulnerable in Lebanese society.

Our usual pattern of interactions while working in the frontlines gets us talking and listening to all sorts of people, like taxi drivers, street vendors, shop clerks, and the concierge in our hotel. That's part of the fun of embedding in a new environment. We inquire about their families and then listen as they relay their personal stories, sometimes finding unexpected similarities in the music we enjoy or the foods we like or the movies we recently saw. In Lebanon, these interactions also yielded, through hushed whispers from our newfound friendly acquaintances, a lurking threat. Unbeknownst to us, or the partner who had introduced us, behind the façade of the reputable civic-minded businessman, Kahlil also allegedly served as the area Hezbollah commander. His humanitarian activities, so instrumental in building trust within the community, earned him connections he could use to store his army's rockets and hide his soldiers in plain sight.

In any MBA international business course, you will learn that the dominant strategy for international expansion is to find a local you can trust to serve as your guide for market entry.[7] These partnerships can be informal, transactional, or even joint, where host country organizations allow for shared ownership. There are tremendous benefits to having partners—they can help navigate hiring a labor force and handling relationships with suppliers, buyers, and governments. The more foreign the environment, the more important the local partner becomes because of something called *cultural distance*, or the degree of difference in the values, norms, and behaviors between two societies. Cultures differ along a number of predictable dimensions, including how accepting it is of unequal power among members of society, how much it prefers masculine values such as assertiveness and achievement, the level of long-term or short-term orientation, the willingness to suppress gratification, and the degree of collectivity. The cultural patterns between Western countries and frontline economies differ in some generalizable and predictable ways. For example, North America and Europe tend to be comparatively intolerant of unequal power distribution while Asian, African, and Latin American countries tend to accept authority embedded in social hierarchy. Northern Europeans and British descendants tend toward individualism as compared with more collectivist Asian, African, and Latin American cultures.

For Western corporations looking to operate in frontline environments with high levels of cultural distance, partnerships are critical. This isn't just about avoiding embarrassing missteps, like fumbling introductions or scheduling meetings late in the day during Ramadan. Local partners often have vital information on how to navigate the environment that would be impossible to ascertain from a distance. However, important choices must be made about which and how many partners to seek out. Two more of our experiences from the field illustrate the potential pitfalls and then set up the possible ways to avoid them.

Business in the Dark in Uganda

Moonlight cascaded through the windows of the small church in the rural outpost of Lamogi, Uganda, gently illuminating the faces of our teammates. "This whole thing, it just doesn't make sense," exclaimed Aida, a law student, as she frustratedly buried her head in her hands. We had spent the day bouncing from one interview to another as our partner took us to survey every part of their operations. We ate a late dinner of beans and matoke (mashed green bananas) with a group of community members and when they all went to bed, we looked for a private place to debrief. Normally we would try to find a bar. But in this tiny village, the church was our best option.

Uganda is one of the least electrified countries in Africa. Just over half of Ugandans have access to electricity. Those living in cities have direct access through the national grid, but many Ugandans rely on diesel generators for power, and some even use expensive kerosene lamps for light. Low-cost rural electrification represents a game changer for development. Beyond the obvious benefits of increased mechanization, manufacturing, improvements to health services, and reduced pollution, electrification has a direct impact on the development of human capital through education.[8] Imagine how just one light bulb in a family home allows students to read and do homework after dark.

Our project had several clients. Our primary partner was an international engineering firm that had designed a novel solar power technology that had the potential to distribute low-cost energy in rural areas. To design ways to commercialize this new technology, a charity provided funding to launch a local Ugandan NGO just for this purpose. It had already established three pilot programs near the northern city of Gulu, where two schools and one community center hosted the solar panels, and the energy was sold both to local businesses and directly to consumers through power hubs where customers paid to recharge their cell phones.

We were hosted by Father John, a local Catholic priest who served as the executive director of the Ugandan NGO. His infectious enthusiasm, bright smile, and local connections were a big part of the success of the pilot locations. As he showed us around a number of potential expansion sites, we filled our notebooks with details about energy consumption and competitor rates. Our team interviewed potential anchor tenants whose usage could smooth out anticipated variability in demand. Most of our team was buzzing about the possibility of how this low cost electricity technology could transform the lives of rural families living beyond the limits of the existing national electrical grid.

But Aida was more skeptical. Sitting in the pews in the dark, we listened as she laid out her observations. Our months-long research indicated that our partner qualified for a significant number of government subsidies designed to support rural energy producers. For the past few days, when Aida had repeatedly asked whether they participated in any of these programs, her questions were met with obfuscation. The standard responses were about technical assessments, safety regulations, steep licensing fees, and other barriers to interacting with government regulators. "It's free money," she declared, "so why are they not taking advantage? Something does not add up." But it wasn't until that night in the church that we put it all together. "The only explanation," Aida said, "is that they are operating without a license. That is not good."

Over the next several days we were able to confirm her suspicions. Our local Ugandan NGO partner was indeed running the solar energy pilot without an electricity license, in direct violation of Ugandan law.[9] We recognized the potential problems that this posed for the engineering firm and set out to determine how these pilots could be brought into compliance with licensing requirements. We documented the risks of current operations: closure if caught and fines. Our team immediately pivoted and outlined the legal process with estimated costs: the best-case scenario required payment of a $7,000 licensing fee and a six-month application timeline. We presented our findings to our partners, excited to have identified the problem before it could cause damage and confident of a feasible way of bringing the operations into legal compliance.

However, our presentation was met with silence. Where we expected gratitude, none was given. Rather, our partners were universally convinced that our recommendations were unnecessary. It was clear that there was a mismatch in expectations and values between our team and our partners.

Such an unexpected reaction forced our team to reconsider all aspects of the project. We genuinely thought we had done everything right in selecting a trusted partner in Uganda. We worked with two international organizations who chose a respected local Catholic priest to lead the Ugandan NGO to run their pilots. We assumed our values and priorities were aligned. It never dawned on us to ask whether the operation was compliant with local laws. And it also never dawned on our partners that we would be so concerned about legality. Our partners had told us the truth, but not the whole truth. It was not that they had intended to hide their noncompliance from us. It was simply that they didn't deem it to be important.

And in fact, there were reasonable factors underlying our partners' attitudes toward legal compliance. Some argued, rationally, that the risk of getting caught was so low that it wasn't worth the effort to apply for the permits (remember that $7,000 licensing fee and six-month application period). Now that they had gone down that road and were already operating without the necessary permits, there were challenges associated with changing direction. Father John was deeply concerned about what would happen to the local businesses that depended on solar energy during the six months they would need to suspend operations to apply for the permits. Our US partners justified their position by deferring to the local Ugandans, assuming that they were more informed on the matter.

However, these justifications emerged only after the licensing non-compliance was uncovered. And as a result, before the pilots' launch, the benefits and drawbacks of legal compliance were not articulated, debated, and weighed systematically to make a well-informed strategic decision. The consequences of making business decisions based on faulty assumptions and incomplete information can be significant. Without weighing the pros and cons and knowingly accepting the risks associated with a given decision, business is operating in the dark.

Ignoring Entrenched Divisions in Rwanda at Business's Peril

In Rwanda in 1994, over the course of one hundred days, Hutus targeted and murdered more than eight hundred thousand Tutsis. At that time, an army of exiled Rwandans then marched into the capital city, Kigali, to end the killing, forcing over a million Hutu genocidaires and civilians to flee to neighboring countries, fearing reprisals. In the shadow of this genocide, the new Rwandan government outlawed references to individuals as either Hutus or Tutsis. The official government position: "There is no ethnicity here. We are all Rwandan."[10]

Prior to Belgian colonization, the Hutu and Tutsi distinction referred to one's occupation: Tutsis owned cattle, while Hutus farmed.

As cattle represented more wealth, Tutsis were considered richer than Hutus. However, as often happens with class distinctions, lines were fuzzy. Those Hutus who earned enough to buy cows became Tutsis, and those Tutsis who lost their cattle became farmers and thus Hutus. The Belgian colonial administration solidified these previously malleable distinctions by issuing identity cards. These divisions became reinforced as the Belgian colonizers favored the minority Tutsi, providing them with access to resources, education, and employment while marginalizing the majority Hutus.

However, erasing these traditional societal divisions is not as easy as proclaiming a government decree. Although historical tribal affiliation wasn't supposed to matter, it was impossible not to notice its impact. A journal entry from one of our team members read, "You know when you are having people over and you don't have time to clean up, so you just shove the mess into the closet and hope the door does not burst open—that's what Rwanda feels like. It's like there is a hidden set of rules that nobody says out loud." We recognized that operating in Rwanda required a particular sensitivity to how market transactions might impact and be impacted by historical cleavages. We relied on our local NGO partners, the program director and her team of extension workers implementing our collaborative agricultural project, to help us navigate this complex landscape.

What we didn't consider was that all Rwandans were subject to these unarticulated forces, even the NGO staff whose programs in the countryside were explicitly aimed at bridging these societal divisions. We noticed that the mood shifted depending on the mix of staff that was present. Sometimes a car ride would be joyful, with people laughing and open. Other times it would feel formal and stiff. They all talked about the importance of unity and transcending historical divisions in public, but in private, their actions betrayed those intentions. After several failed attempts to tactfully inquire about these dynamics and how they might impact our data collection, we realized that we were unlikely to get a straight answer. Instead, we did our best to interact with folks from the widest possible spectrum of Rwandan society to increase the likelihood of uncovering differences in perspectives.

Getting access to a wide swath of Rwandans proved difficult. Our local partner had our activities organized in such a way that we were interacting with only a small subset of their program beneficiaries. Every time we tried to go outside our tightly controlled schedule by setting up our own meetings or engaging in side conversations, we were strongly discouraged. For example, while traveling the road between Kigali and Butare to visit a farmers' group, our car broke down, and we found ourselves on the side of the road with a little extra time on our hands. Seeing an opportunity to gather new perspectives, we wandered off to talk to the farmers tending their nearby rice paddy. Our partner, and even our driver, tried to physically block our way. It seemed that they wanted us to meet only their farmers. We could not figure out the exact source of their resistance. Were they concerned for our safety, as our interest might inflame tensions? Were they worried that we might learn something new that didn't align with what they were telling us? Or were the societal divisions so pervasive that they didn't even realize that they were materially shaping the data we collected?

Although Rwandan society's collective desire was to move beyond the genocide, the behavior we observed on the side of the road made us skeptical that this end goal could be achieved. Our incongruous experiences in the field led us to ask even more questions, as any time that our local partners discouraged us from interacting broadly in society, it cued our skepticism and emboldened our efforts to circumvent these restrictions to gain more diverse information. We leveraged our alumni network to get in touch with Rwandans who were not affiliated with our NGO partner. Every meal, taxi ride, or purchase in a shop became an opportunity to engage in fact finding. We began to pay greater attention to nonverbal cues, body language, and artifacts in our surroundings to triangulate and validate what people were telling us. These additional pieces of data allowed us to notice variation, particularly in who was participating in various government agricultural extension and financial programs. We then were able to map the pattern of social and commercial interactions and document how, despite the unifying rhetoric, few substantive transactions occurred across these historical divisions.

Choosing Frontline Partners

It would be impossible for our teams to work in frontline environments without partners, as we described in Chapter 4. Relationships with the myriad of local actors mitigate both the competitive and the operational risks associated with the frontlines. They do so by providing us with legitimacy, connections, cultural knowledge, and often security. They serve as important thought partners while coproducing any solutions and maintaining a persistent presence that can help us see those programs through to fruition. Nevertheless, partnerships are only as valuable as the quality of information they provide. The three cautionary tales from Lebanon, Uganda, and Rwanda demonstrate the different types of barriers to obtaining reliable information from partners—information businesses need to make strategic decisions.

Although the challenge in Lebanon is the clearest of our three examples, the practical reality of determining the trustworthiness of similarly positioned local partners may prove impossible from the outset. Without verifiable information about partner motivations, many outsiders end up working with whomever is willing. At best, it is left up to chance whether the incentives of your local partners line up with your own. At worst, the lucrative benefit of manipulating outsiders is even more likely to attract those with hidden agendas.

Our experiences in Uganda and Rwanda demonstrate that information quality is not guaranteed, even when working with highly reputable and well-meaning local partners. Differences in values and priorities can lead to an inaccurate or incomplete picture of the local landscape. The challenge is that, as an outsider, you do not know what you do not know. Even when local partners provide what they perceive as good information, it may later be revealed as skewed in some way. For example, a partner may present their own experience or the perspective of the population segment with whom they interact most frequently. Humanitarian NGO staff members may overweight the views of college-educated urban elites because they are more accessible and easier to communicate with than the isolated rural poor. Military groups building bilateral partnerships with foreign armies are likely to be disconnected from the will of civilians, potentially overestimating support for the government. In hindsight, we assumed that our local partners in Uganda would share our tendency to follow rules and laws. That assumption kept us from asking the right questions.

In frontline environments, business decisions based on faulty, inaccurate, or incomplete information can result in significant strategic and operational errors. Or, perhaps even worse, an alliance with a partner with a hidden agenda can lead to reputational risks or other unintended consequences. In adopting a few specific guidelines, businesses can help ensure that the information gathered is more accurate and complete, thereby improving decision making. By partnering broadly and jointly exploring the landscape of opportunities with partners, it is possible to generate a set of associations in frontline environments that will mitigate risk and safeguard investment.

Guidelines to Partner Broadly Through Co-exploration in the Frontlines

Developing trust with any partner is a process, not an event. Building enduring relationships, particularly with partners who contribute vastly different perspectives, often takes time and unfolds while working together. In Chapter 1, we described how we hadn't accounted for the threat of armed middlemen disrupting the market plans we developed with subsistence farmers in Western Uganda. In hindsight, it is not surprising that our partners didn't reveal their fears of these middlemen on our first visit, or even at the beginning of our second visit. We hadn't yet built up enough trust.

It is challenging to convince reputable local partners that they should take the time to get to know outsiders, as many outsiders don't stick around long enough to make the investment worthwhile. Even with the best of intentions, years of international development have sometimes created dysfunctional patterns when it comes to community-outsider relationships. The renowned economist Jeff Sachs, so deeply committed to eradicating extreme poverty (living on less than one dollar per day), argued "the end to poverty" rested on the targeted provision of sufficient aid for the poor to escape poverty traps.[11] Sachs established a number of Millennium Villages across sub-Saharan Africa where he could test his hypothesis that enough money invested into a community would lift it out of poverty. These villages were provided with significant foreign aid to jump-start their drive to self-sufficiency. They were given schools, infrastructure, water, health care, and training on entrepreneurship. But Sachs didn't take the time to develop solutions together with the rural communities his initiatives were meant to serve.

Author Nina Munk spent six years researching and following Sachs. In her book, *The Idealist*, she describes a scene that she argues exemplifies Sachs's approach, one that we argue is doomed to fail.[12] Amid great fanfare, he and his entourage pulled into Dertu, Kenya, in big four-by-four air-conditioned vehicles. A group of villagers had been waiting for hours in the hot sun for their guests to arrive. There were speeches, mostly in English, with greetings and talk of ambitious plans for the future. After ceremonial gift giving and the performance of a traditional dance, the convoy departed. The project, based on the best of intentions, later collapsed with much less fanfare. The regional livestock market, the center of the plan to revitalize the area, was antithetical to the pastoralist traditions of holding onto cattle as wealth. The cattle market failed to entice enough local buyers and sellers, and without them, the expected sustainable economic activity. Even though people didn't take to the market idea, they flocked to the town for the free food and medicine. A shantytown grew up, and when the money ran out, there was no economic activity to pick up the slack. Sachs, Munk argues, did not take the time to learn from the local actors, and unfortunately, in the end, the area was left in worse shape than it had been before he showed up.

Of course, the long process of building relationships often includes a degree of ceremony. However, in our experience, these early public encounters rarely produce our most valued connections. Instead, they set the stage for connections to emerge subsequently, in more private settings. Our most effective long-term partners are often not those who are quick to volunteer—they come from those who initially hang around the sidelines. In fact, we suggest that both sides should approach the development of a partnership with a healthy degree of skepticism. The landscape of poverty alleviation is littered with doomed alliances that failed to live up to their promises: donations of unusable equipment, such as medical machinery that doesn't match the voltage of the country's electrical grid; building of schools and clinics that have grand openings but never get staffed with teachers or nurses; using charitable programs as a way for local officials to funnel cash to their cronies. There is good reason for both sides to take the time to determine trustworthiness and opportunities for mutual gain.

We believe that partnerships should be built at the same place they are going to be executed. Designing development programs in donor offices and universities, far from the communities they are meant to impact, happens rather more often than we would care to admit. This is a common business approach to market entry, where the planning stage is largely completed at headquarters, and partners are selected remotely for their execution capabilities. It is also similar to the way that US Army Special Operations Forces prepare for missions, planning for every potential detail and practicing each maneuver until it becomes routine. We have learned the hard way that in frontline environments it is almost impossible to separate the design and the implementation of any initiative. Or, as our team of soldiers often said, "No plan survives first contact." Imagining and then creating mutually beneficial arrangements together with local partners is both more respectful and enjoys a higher chance of achieving common objectives.

Research on partnerships draws an important distinction between co-exploration, where the focus is on identifying opportunities through learning, discovery, and innovation, and co-exploitation, where the focus is on efficiency, implementation, and execution.[13] We have been most successful when we start with a broad strategic vision for the opportunity but let the details emerge through our interactions with local partners. This co-exploration not only allows us to develop better understanding of the unique context but also helps us understand what might be possible and provides the opportunity to vet partners along the way.

Over time, we have integrated these emerging insights into the ways that we now develop relationships with new partners. The dynamics of our work over the past decade in war-ravaged Mindanao in the Philippines exemplifies how it takes time, effort, and sometimes a few false starts to develop an effective and durable partnership that avoids the many hazards of collaborations. In fact, our current peace-building NGO partner was not the first, or even the second, organization that we partnered with in the Philippines. Committed to serving those emerging from decades of conflict in Mindanao, we launched our initial foray on the island with a faith-based humanitarian organization. Given the sheer inadequacy of capital to rebuild parts of war-torn Mindanao, we also partnered with an international microfinance institution to launch programs to extend credit to farmers. After three years of working with these two partners, we noted that their values were different from ours. Their aim was to support the peace process in Mindanao through enhancing public policy and shaping public discourse in Manila. In contrast, our goal is to work on the ground with communities to launch new businesses and markets that create jobs and establish the economic conditions for growth. We realized that if we were to continue to work in the Philippines, we needed to search for additional partners whose missions were to serve alongside communities to complement and extend these policy-making efforts. We went through our notes from the previous few years and reached out to our contacts in the region to determine the main players in this space.

Although we considered a number of alternative organizations, the track record of impact of this peace-building NGO fit our criteria of an action-oriented partner at the intersection of peace and business in Mindanao. It certainly helped that within the Filipino community of NGOs, people only had compliments for their work. A colleague from the Kroc Institute for International Peace Studies at the University of Notre Dame introduced us to their national director. During our first informal conversation on the sidelines of the UN General Assembly's annual fall meeting in New York City, we were immediately captivated by the respect and compassion that she showed for the former Moro insurgents and their difficulty in transitioning into normal life. It was very hard to resist the temptation to dive headfirst into a full-blown partnership, at least on our end. By contrast, she was much more skeptical of us and the value that we could bring. Nevertheless, we agreed that we would meet the next time we were working on a project in the Philippines.

Little did we know, this meeting was actually a test. A small group of us peeled off from our work in Luzon and flew to Laguindingan airport in Mindanao for what we thought would be high-level discussions with their executive team. They picked us up from the airport, and instead of going to a conference room to discuss their programming, they took us to a rural community to participate in their harvest. We spent the entire day in the fields under a hot sun picking rich red coffee beans alongside former insurgents. We were thrilled. This was exactly the process we use to get to know any new organization and community. But it was only once we clearly passed the test, and they realized that our boots were as dirty as theirs, that individual NGO staff members began to warm to us. From that foundation, we have created an endur-ing partnership, expanding programs to new communities, generating new initiatives, and undertaking major research projects together.

The more local actors you talk to, the more each partner shares, the more likely you will uncover the underlying jugular challenges that characterize the specific frontline environment in which you are look-ing to expand. Employing the information from these local contacts enables businesses to generate novel options to address these challenges and successfully operate in these unfamiliar environments. Yet our experience in Guatemala illustrates the limits of this process as well. Sometimes, having generated new options, businesses must discern when to step aside and respect the communities to make the decisions that directly impact their lives.

The Importance of Trusted Partners: Making Decisions in Guatemala

In 2012 the bishop of Zacapa, Guatemala, Monsignor Rosolino Bianch-etti Boffelli, invited us to his diocese. Although he grew up in Italy, he spoke flawless Spanish and had mastered the local Mayan Quiché lan-guage well enough to translate the New Testament. A man of the peo-ple, tall, grizzled, with short-cropped gray hair, his skin was tanned by prolonged exposure to the sun, and his hands were rough from sow-ing fields and collecting coffee alongside his parishioners. Where other bishops might wear a gold pectoral cross, he wore a simple wooden one.

At a previous posting in Guatemala's Western Highlands, Monsi-gnor Rosolino had helped launch a successful Fair Trade coffee cooper-ative. He looked to replicate this success in Zacapa, confident that the altitude and weather in this even more remote region was equally well suited to growing high-quality arabica coffee. He assembled more than four hundred campesino families, and, thanks to a donation from an Italian NGO, they purchased a drying mill for processing coffee beans. Under his guidance, small coffee farmers in the area sold their first container of Zacapa coffee to Green Mountain Coffee the year before we arrived.

However, despite its initial success, the members of the cooperative had a long way to go to achieve the kind of income that would help them reach the bottom rung of the development ladder. Eager to find new streams of income, Monsignor Rosolino asked our team to investigate whether the cooperative might be able to improve its financial position by producing and selling the fruits that already grew on the land, including bananas whose primary purpose was to provide shade to facilitate coffee growth. As we left the monsignor's rectory, he sent us off with a blessing and the following advice: "Walk in the footsteps of the campesinos," he advised. "Not to understand their challenges, but rather, to understand their hopes and dreams."

We immediately observed why the monsignor was so committed to serving in this remote area. Zacapa is a tough place. For every gun held by the Guatemalan police and military, a hundred were held in private hands. Lawlessness reigned. When leaving Guatemala City, friends warned us to watch out for stray bullets in Zacapa. Our first morning out, we stopped counting when we hit fifty openly displayed guns, and it was not even 10 a.m. It was clear that, behind the tall iron gates of their estates, narco-traffickers essentially ran this wild, isolated valley. Meanwhile, outside those gates, the extreme poverty was visible in the stunting and listlessness of many of Zacapa's malnourished children. It would take more than just one successful coffee sale to alter the trajectory of these family's lives.

Taking heed of the bishop's advice, we spent days in the fields and markets with farmers, and nights poring over our spreadsheet analysis. It initially appeared that selling bananas, in various forms of processing, might be a promising source of revenue. But in the end, the tough mountain geography combined with high cost of transportation across the dispersed farms made these ideas unprofitable. We approached our meeting with the cooperative director nervously, not eager to be the bearers of bad news, but at least heartened that our findings would prevent the cooperative from wasting resources in some convoluted way trying to make a fruit business marginally profitable.

When our team delivered this news, a look of despair appeared on the director's face. "Unfortunately, then we will have to close our doors," he said quietly. We were shocked by this reaction. The cooperative had more than four hundred hardworking families, a shiny new drying mill, and a relationship with Green Mountain Coffee. How could it be in financial trouble this deep?

The director confided in us that the challenge was not assets but cash flow. The coffee cooperative had gone into debt to provide members with fertilizer and pesticides that were to be paid off later. They were now stuck paying off one loan with another, all at exorbitant interest rates. The cooperative would not be able to advance its members the funds to buy fertilizer for the next year's coffee crop, which was anticipated by Green Mountain Coffee. Without fertilizer, there was no way they would meet the order.

Whether or why the bishop and the director intentionally or inadvertently withheld this information from us earlier, this situation is not uncommon in our projects. Sometimes a partner just doesn't know what's important, and sometimes we don't know what to ask of whom. Perhaps the bishop was not aware of the depth of the financial crisis.

Perhaps he believed that we could solve this financial problem and allow him to save face. What we have learned is that this is a key reason to keep bringing new stakeholders into the conversation and to keep talking with everyone. The more each partner shares, the more likely it is that the team will eventually stumble on the underlying problem and find ways to work with the strengths and limitations of the situation.

Armed with this new information, our team regrouped and prepared to change tactics to solve a very different problem for the cooperative. This wasn't about enhancing farmers' incomes or simply restructuring the cooperative's operations to break even in the long term—we needed to find a way for the cooperative to generate cash quickly. One option was to look at monetizing existing underutilized assets. In other words, what did the cooperative already have that it could use to make money?

Although there were many coffee plantations in the area, most lacked a way to process their beans. Not only did the cooperative have the sole large-scale drying mill in the region, but it used the mill for only about one month each year. The rest of the time, the equipment remained idle. The cooperative was sitting on a lucrative asset, and one option was to put it to use. This is the type of pragmatic solution that a business perspective can bring to the table. When we asked the cooperative managers why they hadn't considered this option previously, they told us that they did not perceive the drying mill as an asset to make money from because it was a donation. However, this wasn't the only reason they hadn't monetized the asset. It was well known that some narco-traffickers used coffee crops to launder their illicit gains. The only way to ensure that the asset was not used to benefit drug lords was to leave it idle. If the cooperative were to rent out its equipment, it would likely contribute, albeit indirectly, to strengthening the very drug traffickers that it was trying to break free from.

The monetization of the underutilized asset of the coffee-drying mill was a pragmatic solution to the dire financial situation of the cooperative. But a business perspective could not answer many questions that arose from this option. What was the cooperative's primary goal? To build farmer's incomes to help them look after their families? To help them to escape the threats of the traffickers? Was it worth potentially strengthening drug lords in the short term? The business problem-solving process generated options not previously considered. At this point, it was no longer a business question but an ethical question to be decided by the community and Monsignor Rosolino. They had to discern whether the risk of narco-traffickers using the mill was worth the survival of the cooperative. Only they could answer the moral and ethical questions for themselves. We stepped aside, allowing the other voices at the table to deliberate the decision that would so directly affect their lives.

Bringing business principles to bear on traditionally nonbusiness challenges can turn a problem on its head and generate pragmatic suggestions for how to make money. However, it should not be the only or final perspective that drives a decision. This was the case not only in Zacapa but in many of the examples that we draw on in this book. In Chapter 1, the subsistence farmers in Western Uganda similarly needed to decide whether they would be willing to invite some of the armed middlemen who had been threatening them into their recently launched cooperatives to protect the new market arrangements.

Some have argued that the mere suggestion of these alternatives endangers communities—that the pragmatic solutions that come from business's fresh eye only exacerbate the problems facing poor communities, trading one negative consequence for another. We recognize that the stark reality of daily life in frontline environments often requires communities to make many compromises to survive. However, business cannot and should not bear the weight of these decisions. Its role is not to impose business values on difficult situations faced by frontline communities. Those choices are theirs alone to make, but together, with a greater diversity of perspectives at the table, we can give them more options to consider.

In the end, Monsignor Rosolino and community leaders, having weighed the options, implications, and associated moral quandaries, decided to rent out their coffee-drying equipment to the neighbors. The cooperative staved off bankruptcy, made the next coffee sale to Green Mountain Coffee (who remained unaware of these financial issues), and continues to provide a means for the farmers and their families to improve their livelihoods. The cooperative, as a business, was not an end in itself. It was a means toward much more critical ends—an opportunity for the poor to lift themselves from poverty—and this decision allowed for that work to continue.

The stakes of operating in the frontlines are immense. Given their cycles of poverty and violence, they pose a great deal of uncertainty for business investors. Collaborations are likely to illuminate very different priorities, values, and motivations across actors. Our experiences in Lebanon, Uganda, and Rwanda highlight not only how partners with goodwill can sometimes still withhold critical data or provide biased input, but also how local partners can pursue hidden agendas very counter to our own. The story of the cooperative in Zacapa illustrates why it is so essential to work with multiple local partners who can weigh the trade-offs and navigate the difficult daily demands imposed by the frontlines. As a result, to drive international expansion effectively, we argue to develop a broad set of partnerships, contrary to conventional wisdom that dictates creating deep ties with a small number of local partners. Not only does the traditional approach increase the likelihood of risky business decisions based on missing or flawed information; it also may place vital community decisions in the wrong hands.

When businesses intentionally seek out different perspectives by building contacts that span generational, geographical, socioeconomic, ethnic, and religious divides and cultivate trust slowly, they can operate more effectively in the frontlines. Not only will they be better able to identify, design, and develop opportunities that will benefit all parties, but these relationships will be invaluable in steering through the complex sociopolitical and ethical questions that are invariably going to emerge. Despite the extra work, don't cut short the effort of investigating the myriad of local actors and cultivating a wide range of allies. The benefit of safeguarding investment through enduring, broad-based local partnerships is well worth the effort. Indeed, the hushed whispers of your new partners may be all that stands between those with hidden agendas, missing perspectives, and misguided strategic decisions and you.

Identifying and engaging with these nontraditional partners is only the beginning of developing durable relationships. Next comes the hard work of building the trust that facilitates the interactions that yield so much fruit. How can businesses turn their early contacts and conversations into lasting partnerships, especially when community elders, government officials, or NGO staff will likely not share your same motivations? The next chapter lays out approaches to transform initial shared ideas and experiences into mutually beneficial relationships.

CHAPTER 7

Imagine and Create Common Ground

*Convening and considering a variety of perspectives is key to copro-
ducing creative solutions you cannot access on your own.*

H istorically, Vietnamese society has called people with mental or physical disabilities *đứa trẻ vô dụng*, which is variously translated as "useless children," "the lost ones," or "nonproductive."[1] Families are often embarrassed by these children and hide them away, denying them an education, training, or other means of developing as a person. Unfortunately, because of leftover ordinance from the Vietnam War (1955–1975), as well as the consequences of the US military's use of the toxic chemical Agent Orange, Vietnam has some of the highest rates of disability in the world.[2] Approximately 5.2 million people in Vietnam live with disabilities, with very few social programs to support them.

Programs for this stigmatized group almost never got off the ground because of other legacies of the war. Even two generations afterward, there remained strong anti-American and anti-Catholic sentiment across the country. People name their children Lenin and Marx and their dogs Nixon and Kissinger. The Communist government still actively persecutes the country's small Catholic community, as it both represents the legacy of French colonial rule and because the church was among the most ardently anti-Communist institutions during the Vietnam War. It does so by arresting and appropriating land from both the Catholic Church and poor Catholic farmers, deeming them, in Marxist terms, as "counterrevolutionaries." It is astonishing, then, that the Communist government of Vietnam; Catholic Relief Services (CRS), the international humanitarian organization supported by the Catholic community in the United States; and the US Agency for International Development (USAID), the international development agency of the United States federal government, worked together to create programs to support the country's many disabled people.

That these former adversaries became unlikely allies illustrates the way that business can create common ground with even the most unusual partners. In its ninth five-year plan (2010–2015), the Vietnamese government made care for disabled children and youth a national priority. At the time, CRS was a widely acknowledged leader in the design of programs to support people with disabilities in achieving their potential. CRS was also a long-standing implementing partner of USAID for health care, disaster relief, and development programs in nearly one hundred countries around the world. Early tentative conversations between Vietnamese government officials and CRS staff were off the record and low key, held on the sidelines of international conferences during coffee breaks between sessions. These exploratory discussions led to meaningful dialogue regarding the opportunity to better serve this vulnerable community. The leaders of all three organizations found the courage to transcend their differences. Together, they solicited input from leaders within the Vietnamese disabled community on their needs and priorities to help design education and employment programs for disabled youth.

Collaborations are tricky by nature. Each group had its own agendas and stakeholders. Leaders from each organization had to be extremely clear eyed about each other's needs and deal breakers. As they cautiously developed a rapport, it became clear each brought different skills and assets to the table, and consequently, they recognized that they needed each other to achieve their goals. CRS came to the table with the knowledge necessary to design innovative programming and the people—psychologists, social workers, teachers—already experienced in serving the disabled. As the US government's international development agency, USAID contributed funding and support. The Vietnamese government brought its commitment to change the national legal and administrative framework necessary to support the disabled. Critically, local leaders of the disabled community contributed an understanding of what they actually needed.

They were also very careful to jointly circumscribe the boundaries of this collaborative project so that potential major ideological disagreements would not trigger the collapse of the process. One example was when Catholic Relief Services and USAID agreed to be more muted about their contributions so as not to unnecessarily antagonize members of the Vietnamese Communist Party who condemned collaborations like this one. But throughout the project, each partner listened and brought honesty into their regular dialogue with the others. They also needed to discern when to give ground, develop consensus approaches, overcome the inevitable obstacles, and drive the changes needed within their own organizations and systems to make it work—none of which they could do without agreeing upon clear boundaries in their relationship.

Innovative collaborations like the one in Vietnam begin with a glimpse of a different and better future that captures the imagination of the leaders of all the partner organizations. Without that inspiration, organizations won't be able to stomach the hard work required to jointly turn their shared idea—something they each can't accomplish on their own—into a reality. A shared vision of caring for a neglected group of people gave these unlikely collaborators the courage to embark on this journey together, but then came the long and challenging process of developing empathy. They practiced being flexible and civil to one another while also keeping their goal in sight—to work toward the betterment of the lives of the physically and mentally disabled. The results: together the partners launched fifty specialized schools and tailored vocational training programs across the country that every year now help more than ten thousand children and young adults with disabilities to live their lives to the fullest.

The world's toughest problems rarely respect sectoral or disciplinary boundaries, and neither do their effective solutions. Solving them requires nontraditional partnerships that can navigate vastly different backgrounds, circumstances, and cultures. Understanding the landscape of players, their needs, and interests; approaching others with humility; starting open-ended conversations; and consciously adopting a nonjudgmental position are critical elements to developing the relationships needed to get the work done. We suggest that this process rests on listening closely and following up on areas of common interest to coproduce solutions that all partners have a stake in. Collaborators must not only learn to leverage the unique skills, knowledge, and contributions of each partner, but also agree upon ways to protect the potential areas of collaboration from the inevitable disagreements.

Why begin the chapter on imagining and creating common ground with Vietnamese Communists, CRS, and USAID? There certainly was no direct business implication in this story. Nevertheless, we chose this example for its extremes. In the end, the Communist government did not need to be any less communist. CRS didn't need to be any less faith based. And USAID did not need to rewrite the history of the Vietnam War. Yet all worked together diligently and extensively to launch educational and vocational training programs to address the needs of the disabled. If it is possible for adversaries to overcome the legacy of war to build a partnership, then it is certainly possible for businesses to develop vibrant collaborations with the myriad of actors in the frontlines.

Guidelines to Imagine Common Ground, Develop Relationships, and Articulate Boundaries

To move a vision forward in a way that is mutually beneficial and truly coproduced by all partners through their participation, you must foster deep relationships among people with very different backgrounds. As many of the stories in this book have illustrated, the path to creative solutions requires sitting under a mango tree, at the dinner table, or even in a brothel, and engaging in open-ended conversations. When you listen to other people's stories without judgment or preconception, something important happens. When we sat with armed middlemen in Uganda or pimps in the Philippines, we didn't imagine we would have much sympathy for them. However, sharing stories of love, loss, and hope for our families allowed us to find our common humanity. These encounters form the beginnings of a shared language and understanding that eventually allow for the genesis of trust and genuine regard, perhaps even affection.

In fact, finding this common humanity among avowed adversaries represented the essential ingredient to the success of the project in Vietnam: Trinh was the Communist official who quietly organized the initial conversations, cajoled colleagues in the Communist Party to support the initiative, chaired the meetings of the partners, and determinedly kept the process on track. We found out later that Trinh and his wife's teenage daughter was severely disabled. This family circumstance enabled Trinh to connect—at a deeply personal level—with the Americans dedicated to improving the lives of disabled children like his daughter. These similarities create the common ground that underpins true collaboration and fosters innovative solutions. And today, after many years of medical therapy and participation in these newly launched vocational programs, Trinh's daughter has fulfilled her wish to become a caregiver to other disabled children.

Building these connections takes time, which doesn't always come naturally for fast-moving business. To benefit from nontraditional collaborations, business leaders must play the long game. Then they must have the patience and insight to provide cover so that teams can draw members from different backgrounds and organically create a working rhythm based on mutual respect. As trust among collaborators grows, the relationships can withstand the early stumbles that inevitably occur during such a challenging process.

A key component of these collaborations is clearly articulating boundaries to avoid triggering underlying and intractable value conflicts. Actors have to put aside their often substantial differences to find ways to work together on issues of shared concern. Sometimes partners will do or say things we don't agree with, but by being committed to the larger vision and erecting clear and agreed-upon boundaries, we can respect each other's individual missions. When collaborators can avoid the pitfalls of unproductive relationship conflict, they can effectively leverage their diverse perspectives and experiences to work toward their shared objectives.[3]

We have filled this book with many examples of our unusual and successful partnerships with a variety of actors around the globe. However, we believe that the best lessons have come from our most gut-wrenching failures. Despite years of practice and the best of intentions, we have failed multiple times to pull off collaborations among cross-sector players. The upside of diversity is innovation, but the downside of diversity is that sometimes it is just too difficult to manage, as you'll see from these stories from Ghana and our work with the US military.

Failing to Build on Mutual Interest in Ghana

Ghana is a prototypical frontline country. Despite sustained economic growth catapulting the nation into the World Bank's upper-middle-income classification, the mostly Muslim population living in the arid north has not seen the fruits of these economic gains. As a result of this reclassification, many international humanitarian organizations working in Ghana have faced declining funding, as donors prioritize countries with perceived greater need. In 2014, a leading international humanitarian NGO recruited us to investigate the possibility of partnering with multinational corporations as an avenue to replace those donor funds. We immediately thought of Newmont Mining (whom you met in Chapter 2) as a potential partner for the NGO.

Newmont's sprawling operations in Ghana stretched across a terri-tory the size of Los Angeles. With two enormous gold mines, Newmont generated nearly 10 percent of Ghana's exports, 5 percent of its total base of foreign direct investment, and 1.3 percent of the gross domestic product.[4] But more importantly, Newmont's approach to foreign direct investment in frontline environments rested on deep embeddedness in the local community. It had launched the Newmont Ahafo Devel-opment Foundation (NADF), specifically dedicated to developing the underserved area around the mine. Jointly governed by community members and Newmont executives, NADF received $1 for every ounce of gold sold from the mine and 1 percent of the net profits made in the country, amounting to more than $2 million each year. It reinvested these funds locally, based on community priorities. It had already built several primary schools, launched a health clinic, funded educational scholarships, and created a microfinance lending program to help local entrepreneurs launch new ventures. We wondered whether Newmont's and the NGO's values might align to form a fruitful partnership. The NGO would have new funding while Newmont could maximize their impact in the community.

We found a specific opportunity for collaboration by comparing the microfinance programs of each organization, both of which pro-vided small loans to local start-ups. Although the NGO had no lending program in the communities around the mine, in other areas in Ghana and around the world, it achieved excellent results. It boasted experi-enced personnel with global experience. Its offices were humming with activity as entrepreneurs and staff worked together on applications for exciting new ventures. In contrast, NADF had no dedicated offices, and the lending committee, chaired by the mine's general manager, met once a month. The data supported our initial impressions: for every

$1,000 annual investment in their comparable microfinance programs, NADF reached between 6 and 7 beneficiaries, while the NGO programs reached approximately 750.

This gap in efficacy is not surprising. NADF was formed with good intentions, but Newmont is, at heart, a mining company, not a humanitarian service provider. It specializes in operating billion-dollar mines, not twenty-five-dollar loans. By contrast, the international NGO was a true leader and innovator in the field of microlending and microfinance. Globally, it had more than one hundred thousand active microfinance participants across fifty countries. We thought that if Newmont outsourced this work to the NGO, it could increase its impact in the communities around the mine. The NGO would have a corporate partner providing a new source of funds, thereby expanding their reach into a new area of the country. Given our relationship with both organizations, if we could play matchmaker, both parties could benefit.

To encourage the budding new relationship, we suggested that both parties see each other in action. We accompanied the NGO's directors for West Africa and Ghana on the fifteen-hour bus ride from Accra north to the Newmont mine to see firsthand the mining operations and all the work done to embed them into the surrounding community. The mine's South African general manager, who also led the foundation, greeted us at the gate and personally gave us a tour. That evening under the starry sky, before retiring to our modest barracks constructed from shipping containers, the general manager hosted us for a braai, a South African barbecue. The NGO's country director and the general manager compared their common experiences of working across the continent in places like the Congo and Liberia. The next day, we visited the foundation's development programs, where we observed the warmth with which the village elders greeted the general manager. Although the NADF programs may have been run less effectively, what the visit made clear was the shared deep commitment by both Newmont and the NGO to improving the lives of poor rural Ghanaians.

The visit felt like a success.

A week later we regrouped in Accra, where our team presented a detailed proposal to both organizations, eager to broker a deal. We were worried about sensitivity on Newmont's part, because the numbers highlighted the stark inefficiency of NADF's microfinance program. However, to our surprise, the Newmont executives brushed off the criticism and immediately grasped the opportunity, peppering us with questions like, How much would the NGO charge to take their microfinance program off their hands? What was their ability to scale? When could we begin?

In contrast, the response from the NGO leadership was tepid. Unlike Newmont, who is accustomed to outsourcing a variety of activities, the NGO didn't have any experience in this type of arrangement with a for-profit corporation. No businesses had ever tried to outsource a program to them. In the normal course of events, NGOs do contract activities with other NGOs and thus have a well-developed means of negotiating memorandums of understanding to do so, but this one had never sold their services to a for-profit bidder on the open market. Furthermore, this NGO, like many others, was used to designing their own programs based on their own priorities and those of the communities they served. NGO staff were unaccustomed to internalizing the objectives of outsiders. The NGO's lack of experience manifested in significant rigidity. The staff had no internal guidelines and protocols on how to proceed. They asked many more internally focused questions, like, How might they price such an arrangement? How would they structure the contract? Who would oversee the project? How would they decide how to spend the additional funds? What types of reporting procedures would be needed?

Although our team perceived none of these problems to be deal breakers, lack of experience was not the only barrier. The NGO staff could not see past the overall extractive industry's notorious disregard for both safety and the environment to recognize Newmont's hard-earned reputation for commitment to labor safety, protection of the environment, and zero tolerance for corruption. We tried to help them see how working with NADF was similar to their usual contracts with other NGOs. Nonetheless, their reservations about the partnership persisted. What would their board think? Was it within their scope to accept payment for services from a corporation? Given their mission, could they even consider working with a mining company? How would this impact their reputation?

In the end, what seemed to our team to be an obvious opportunity for both sides never materialized. On the one hand, Newmont was ready to partner but was accustomed to making deals with a handshake and ironing out the details later. It was unable to recognize the differences between its process and the NGO's and did not adjust to the slower and more cautious pace of decision making. The NGO, on the other hand, didn't have a process to run innovative ideas up the flagpole and thus could not begin to negotiate terms, which in itself would have jump-started the process of developing trust in the relationship. Instead, they deliberated internally for three months before presenting the idea to their board. By that time, Newmont had moved on to other priorities. In the end, they couldn't come together despite their clear common interest.

The lesson from our experience in Ghana is that even when you have a great idea—one that represents clear mutual benefit—translating that common ground into progress toward new mutually beneficial arrangements that transcend differences is hard. By their very nature, for-profit businesses and nonprofit agencies speak different languages, work toward different timelines, and conduct different internal review and decision-making processes. In hindsight, our matchmaking tripped up both on the critical first step of imagining common ground and in understanding the needs and interests of the local actors. We may have started with a great idea that the potential partners seemed interested in. But one good visit does not make a relationship. One could fault the NGO for being too slow to do the deal, but from another perspective, one could fault the mining executives for not investigating and understanding the needs of the NGO. For any partnership, it takes two to tango. Without investment in a shared vision and putting in the time to understand each other, the potential collaboration collapsed.

Encountering Structural Barriers to Ongoing Collaboration with the US Military

"It would be easier to get authorization for a drone strike in the Middle East to kill an American citizen than to get authorization for deploying US soldiers on a conflict prevention mission." Those were the exasperated words coming from the speakerphone in the center of our team room at the University of Notre Dame. We were on a conference call with eight Judge Advocates General (JAGs) from four different Commands, and they were pulling the plug on our ongoing collaboration with the US Army Special Operations Command that had deployed our joint teams on missions in Senegal and Honduras, as described in Part I.[5]

How did we get to this point? With two successful deployments of joint soldier-civilian projects and three long years of cultivating this collaboration, we couldn't believe that it could be terminated so suddenly and decisively. Our whole team of soldiers and civilians were crushed. In hindsight, we can identify several reasons why this partnership started off well but eventually was not permitted to expand.

It was initially successful because everyone involved shared a vision—that conflict prevention in priority regions was critical to national security—and the shared belief that we could jointly innovate a series of pragmatic economic and security interventions that could improve USASOC's capabilities in this domain. Our success was also the product of a great deal of time developing relationships, especially with our Special Forces soldiers, intentionally learning each other's needs and redlines. This required the team to negotiate a delicate balance to focus on our shared objectives and not on what made us different. For example, we never asked questions about the crates of missiles and grenades in the Special Forces safe houses in West Africa and Central America, and in return they kept quiet when we inevitably made missteps related to security. Finally, we built relationships up the chain of command and had a series of commanders who carefully created conditions for our success by designing missions around objectives that lent themselves to the economic problem solving and security strengths of our teams.

What we missed was that for collaborations to persist in the long term, it is not enough to work well with a subunit of a partner; eventually the collaboration must connect to the whole organization. This requires partners to be willing to not just create space for activities at its periphery but to substantively change their own systems and organizations to institutionalize these activities. Business, by its very nature, excels at this. Its stock and trade is innovating at the periphery and incorporating those innovations quickly based on market signals. By contrast, the US military is one of the world's largest bureaucracies; it does not adapt quickly. Eventually, the bureaucracy's inability to modify internal systems curtailed our collaboration in several critical ways.

First, we didn't account for how authorities are granted in the US military for ongoing deployments. For the past two decades, through the annual National Defense Authorization Act, Congress has authorized the US military to take on new roles, including counterterrorism, counterinsurgency, and counter-narcotics missions. Although nothing in the thousand-page legislation prohibited conflict prevention missions, nothing explicitly permitted them either, leaving the project exposed to termination at any moment. We falsely assumed that doing good work and getting results on the ground was enough to propel an initiative forward. Our joint team of soldiers and civilians alike missed the fact that we needed to combine our work on the ground during deployments with complementary activities back at command headquarters. We needed to reshape the broader governing framework in which these deployments were conducted to ensure their longevity.

Second, business leaders and military commanders make decisions on different time scales. Although there is a caricature that business does not take the long view and focuses only on financial results for the next quarter, in reality, business must make long-term decisions to build operations that last. To illustrate, when Newmont Mining makes an investment in a new gold mine, its business trajectory can easily last for twenty years, given the lifetime of the mine. Yet to remain profitable, businesses must also be willing to pull the plug on sunk cost investments if they do not see tangible results in a reasonable time frame.

In the US military, by contrast, commanders transition every two to three years. And with these frequent transitions, so do the priorities of the command. We didn't account for how quickly and drastically priorities could change. Commanders have a fair amount of leeway in operationalizing their intent or objectives. This fact worked to our advantage when Lieutenant General Cleveland was in command, as his vision to defend US national security by, with, and through local partners that influence conditions in frontline environments aligned with our approach. However, his long-term stability-oriented measures differed from other commanders' more kinetic priorities in dealing with adversaries. In many of our other long-term partnerships we have been able to anticipate and manage succession challenges. However, because of the way the military promotes and rotates its officers, it is nearly impossible to incorporate and influence the next line of commanders before they assume command. As a result, our initiative was also a casualty of shifting military leadership and priorities.

Finally, we didn't effectively frame our initiative within the dominant ways of conducting military missions such that it could be institutionalized in command headquarters. The military is the embodiment of protocol and predictability. Missions are prioritized, practiced, and planned down to every excruciating detail. By contrast our projects were much more open ended and ambiguous. We outlined our mission in ambitious but vague steps: go out into the community, meet people, talk to them, and identify potential leaders. Then convene and coordinate disparate initiatives that could build momentum toward economic opportunity and eventually nudge a territory toward greater stability as local residents have livelihoods and a greater stake in peace. The soldiers we worked with directly embraced this process, bragging how our work was "so far off the farm" compared with their traditional missions. We were also thrilled to tell anyone who would listen how different we were from business as usual for the military. We should have realized that ideas as revolutionary as ours can often be perceived as subversive and generate backlash. We focused so much on our innovations that we didn't consciously and systematically draw connections to how the military already operated. As a result, we missed the opportunity to cement our efforts into well-established processes that underpin the military's training, planning, and deployment.

It could also be that Lieutenant General Cleveland's bold vision of competing for influence in the "Human Domain" and our initial collaboration with USASOC were simply a decade too early. Recently, a new set of commanding Generals have approached us to explore potential partnerships. In 2022, the National Defense Authorization Act appropriated funds to inaugurate a new dedicated military institute to study and train US armed forces in irregular warfare, competitive statecraft, and conflict prevention. Indeed, in many ways, this new institute is already behind and will need to catch up with the rapidly changing facts on the ground: our adversaries have figured out how to compete effectively to influence frontline environments by coupling military action with social programs and economic initiatives. Remember Khalil, the alleged Hezbollah commander we met in Chapter 6 who influences his community in South Beirut through his vast network of business initiatives? It is also hard to ignore the way that China has leveraged large business investments in frontline environments to influence national governments and societies.[6] Freshly paved roads and new buildings are popping up all over the globe, complete with large signs that read, "Brought to You by the Chinese People."

This time, collaboration with another generation of commanding Generals will have to start with conversations about how to institutionalize our innovations. We will have to directly address the structural differences in our approaches to plan for the long-term success of our collaboration. This will include issues of command changes and mission authorities, ways to incorporate our initiatives into existing systems of soldier education and pre-mission training, and outreach to business in the development of theater security plans. We are convinced that to counter our adversaries effectively in the evolving geopolitical landscape will require that business and the military work together to develop innovative strategies. However, to have a lasting impact, such novel initiatives must not only succeed in the field but also transform the systems and organizations of the partners themselves.

At the time, what was lost was the chance to bring this conflict prevention approach with the Special Forces soldiers to other unstable parts of the world. Nevertheless, our joint team deployments in Senegal and Honduras successfully changed the conditions on the ground in both regions. Our projects identified multiple stakeholders who were committed to working together to retake control of neighborhoods and territory from adversaries. We launched processes that coordinated disparate initiatives to systematically dismantle the many obstacles to economic growth. The momentum created by these processes increased security, reduced costs, and thus, modified the risk-return calculations on investments just enough to encourage new business expansion. Because of their inherent market discipline and pragmatism, these newly launched businesses have continued to operate, serve customers, create jobs, and ultimately, foster stability.

It's Hard, but Not Impossible

Common ground is not something that simply exists. Nor is it something that manifests automatically from shared ideas and experience. We must imagine it, create it, and then continuously work to maintain it. With commitment and a strong shared vision, even groups who are typically adversaries can use this process to partner toward greater ends. Unfortunately, today it seems that members of our society do not easily interact with those with different values. Most people spend time in an echo chamber, hearing only thoughts they agree with, talking only to people who agree with them, and reading only what supports their point of view.

To be successful with this process, it is essential to rediscover the value of dialogue. We must be willing to engage in conversation with those whose perspectives, life experiences, and opinions are different from our own. This must be done with curiosity but without judgment. As we gain new insights through such experiences, we must reflect, reevaluate, and even sometimes change our own perspectives. In honest conversation with those who are different from us, we must look for commonalities where we can cocreate potential solutions to problems that affect us all.

The personal mindsets and capabilities needed to navigate this path of partnership are not something you learn in elementary school or even at home. Skills like communication, empathy, intellectual rigor, audacity, and optimism, so central to working in new and uncertain environments, are consciously cultivated through practice, deep reflection, conversation, meditation, and other religious, spiritual, and personal development work through the years. We take inspiration in these encouraging words from St. Augustine of Hippo, "Let us, on both sides, lay aside all arrogance. Let us not, on either side, claim that we have already discovered the truth. Let us seek it together as something which is known to neither of us. For only then may we seek the truth, lovingly and tranquilly, if there be no bold presumption that it is already discovered and possessed."[7]

Conducting business in the frontlines rests on cultivating a broad set of trusted partnerships. Indeed, these local partners provide the diversity of knowledge and experience so critical to effective decision making. But how can you make the most of these relationships? In such unfamiliar circumstances, how do you even know what questions to ask and what information you may need? During the normal course of business, companies now have exponentially more data at their disposal, and their traditional expansion strategies certainly depend on thorough analysis of mounds of information. Yet the complete lack of official economic statistics and data characterizes the often overlooked and isolated frontline markets. To be effective in this arena, how can businesses overcome the wholesale absence of the data to which they are accustomed? The next chapter describes the approaches businesses can adopt to generate actionable data and analysis that can accelerate their expansion into the frontlines.

CHAPTER 8

Dirty Boots and Open Hearts

Immersive experience, feeling, and listening are the foundation to gather data and surface business opportunities.

Trash pickers in Padang, Indonesia, start very early in the morning because the competition is fierce. Every night, when wealthy households are fast asleep, the staff cleans up and sets out the trash before closing up the house. However, instead of taking the garbage out to a bin to be picked up at the curb on a certain schedule by city workers, trash is either burned or placed in very thin plastic bags tied in a double knot and hung on a hook from the brick or wooden fence surrounding the compound, facing the street. These bags full of trash (and possible treasure) represent extra income for informal trash pickers who sort and sell metal and plastic to recyclers. At each house, they tear into the thin bags, spilling their contents onto the dirt. They collect only the perfect plastic that can be sold to the highest-paying recyclers who will then turn it into tiny pellets before selling it to manufacturers. The rest of the garbage, mostly food scraps and wet paper products, are left where they fall, littering the ground.

Although informal trash picking is difficult, tedious, and stigmatized, it is not the domain of the most indigent. Most trash pickers are women seeking supplemental income who have other jobs during the day in markets or working in the fields. On school holidays, they bring their children, who run back and forth around the streets, kicking discarded fruit around as if it were a soccer ball while their mothers work. Many spend hours on public transportation to travel to these wealthy areas to collect trash, bringing soap and a towel to wash themselves after work so as not to offend other bus passengers with the smell of their trade. They lock their wheelbarrows behind a shed and hope they will be there the next day. Although they are not formally organized, many know one another, careful to stay only in their negotiated territory, and look after one another's turf to ensure that no newcomer threatens their earnings.

Padang is the largest city on the western coast of the island of Sumatra. Before the 2009 earthquake, Padang was highly regarded as Indonesia's cleanest city, receiving awards eighteen years in a row for its cleanliness and appearance. However, as the city struggled to rebuild following the earthquake, waste management became an afterthought. Sadly, the city's current waste problems make it more vulnerable to natural disasters, as trash-clogged open sewers increase flooding and spread disease. Everyday, six hundred tons of waste are produced in the city, two hundred of which go uncollected by city services. The city owns twenty-nine dump trucks to collect trash from littering and informal dumping sites and thirty Ambrol trucks to pick up and drop off the three hundred dumpsters placed around the city.

Working for the trash collection agency, Diet Kantong Plastik (DKP), demands a seven-day work schedule and pays low wages. Our team joined a four-person crew in the predawn hours for several days of garbage collection. The driver of the dump truck and informal crew chief, Joyo, welcomed us to the job. Joyo might have been either forty or sixty years old, his weathered face and gnarled hands obscuring his true age. Two garbage collection veterans, Bimo and Ismaya, rode on top of the garbage truck and were training their fourth crewmate, eighteen-year-old Citro. As we rode on top of the truck, Bimo and Ismaya began to train our team as well, showing us how to dig through the collected waste to salvage any recyclable materials before emptying the truck's contents in the landfill. Despite the physically taxing work under hot and humid conditions, the crew laughed and joked throughout the long day. They shared an easy sense of camaraderie and pride in doing honorable work.

We spent similarly challenging and enlightening days with various actors across the value chain: pushing a wheelbarrow with informal trash collectors, scouring plastic with entrepreneurs who cleaned and sorted recyclables, and working in large warehouses the size of football fields filled with sorted recyclables where medium sized processors aggregate and package them for sale. These experiences allowed us to document the multistep industry value chain and associated economics of garbage collection, particularly around recycling plastic.

Selling recycled plastic is an important source of income. For Joyo and his crew, they rely on it to supplement their income. In fact, most days selling the recyclables almost doubles their salary. Each day they drive their route to about eight dumpsters for which they are responsible. Sometimes when they arrive at a site, they find a dumpster overflowing with trash. Other times they find the dumpster with only a tiny bit of garbage. The worst days are when they arrive to find that the once full dumpster is mostly empty, its twenty cubic yards of contents spilled over the side by people scavenging for things to sell. On those days, not only do they fall behind schedule, picking up the mess, making it more likely for the next dumpster to have the same problems, but all the valuable recyclables have already been picked over.

The informal trash collectors and the city garbage workers sell their scavenged materials to a series of small businesses, or agents, who transform them into incrementally more valuable items, then selling them to larger recycling processors. Starting with small agents, they negotiate with the individual collectors for their raw materials and do a first pass at cleaning and sorting. Small agents work out of their homes, with white burlap sacks filled with each color of cleaned plastic piled as high as their roofs. Larger agents often avoid the drudgery of cleaning, getting plastic inputs for their processing and transformation by buying them from smaller agents. Chinese processors used to purchase all their output, but that market now has its own trash processing system. Without guaranteed major buyers, the market is volatile, with prices varying from day to day. It is important to sell only when the price is favorable. Like the city garbage crews, these small business proprietors are proud of their work. They view themselves as entrepreneurs, employing neighbors to work alongside them as they painstakingly scrub, sort, and package the single-serving containers that fuel day-to-day lives. These are but three of the more than twenty steps that a single piece of trash can take as it moves through the entire value chain from household discard to a potential sale to end customers who then then put the plastic to new use.

Our partner, Mercy Corps, an international humanitarian organization, recruited our team to investigate better ways to commercialize trash. Before we traveled to Indonesia, we had done our homework. We had researched TakaTaka Solutions in Kenya as a model of social enterprises and Waste Impact in India and Belo Horizonte in Brazil and how both had reorganized the informal trash collection sector in their respective countries. Each has redesigned waste management in poor neighborhoods, finding new ways to organize collection services or inventing new uses for trash in products for sale. We had investigated the various ways that countries around the world process trash to create compost, biogas, pelletized plastic, and even handicrafts. However, it was only by getting our boots dirty with deep immersion into the literal mess in Padang, thanks to the gracious welcome of Joyo and his garbage truck crew, that we recognized both the complexity and the opportunity that existed. After days spent riding on top of garbage trucks, pushing wheelbarrows filled with recyclables over uneven streets, and scrubbing dirt from crumpled plastic water bottles, we could see how all the activities in the value chain fit together to create the overall ecosystem of collectors, agents, and customers.

Immersive and Inductive Data-Gathering Approach

Getting our boots dirty is one of the critical elements of our process to evaluate frontline opportunities. We immerse ourselves in the day-to-day lives of those we hope to serve. Like Holly with her backpack of coffee beans standing on the mountainside in Guatemala in Chapter 3, this immersion enables us to experience firsthand the daily challenges that business can help overcome. Thoughtful immersive experiences lay the foundation not only for critical data collection but also subsequent understanding and shared empathy. We accomplish our data gathering through a variety of methods, including interviews and focus groups, creating profiles of customers and competitors, organizing surveys and questionnaires, and engaging in the activities of everyday life. The magic of this data-gathering approach is that it is not rigidly prescribed but rather leaves it to the problem solver to proceed in a nonlinear and iterative manner as they gain more information and insight.

However, this approach is not without predictable pitfalls. One in particular is the challenge of sampling, or accessing the appropriate variety of informants. Without careful attention to purposeful sampling, any innovations or solutions run the risk of being based inadvertently on skewed information. In fact, we suggest that this error is particularly likely in unfamiliar environments. As we suggest in Chapter 6, the first line of contact in the frontlines often takes the form of whatever local partner is most easily identified and accessed. Although these partners can be a vast source of valuable information, they represent only a small subset of perspectives that are likely to make up diverse and fragmented societies. For example, although we work largely with very well-intentioned NGO partners whose mission is to serve vulnerable populations, most operate from their headquarters in urban centers far from many of their program beneficiaries. Even when we have worked with partners who are located in frontline environments, they are often separated from the harsh challenges of daily life, living in secure enclaves with drivers and housekeepers and sending their children to private schools.

For example, Mercy Corps' Indonesian headquarters was in Jakarta, far from the daily realities of the informal trash workers in Padang. Mely, the cheerful program coordinator who initially had the idea of commercializing trash, was the only staff member in West Sumatra and had to oversee all the programs in the region. She spent most of her days coordinating with government officials and other NGOs in air-conditioned offices. Important work. But far from the humid streets where informal trash collectors, garbage workers, and recycling agents spend their days. During our project she introduced us to regional businesses, the DKP, and other government agencies. She had an amazing network of contacts that we were able to leverage to get introductions to informal trash workers. However, when it came to the type of fine-grained data that we needed to understand the trash ecosystem, she was no more an expert than we were. Together, we labored alongside trash workers, learning and developing insights while mapping the entire trash value chain.

Sparked by Mely's entrepreneurial observations, our early ideas turned into a garbage collection and recycling franchise system. The Rockefeller Foundation provided a multimillion-dollar grant to launch and then scale the system. This initial seed capital established a system of small franchises based on designated recycling collection sites and routes, providing training and implementing safety protocols. These franchises did not displace the existing informal system of trash workers but incorporated hundreds of them into a predictable and safe occupation. Once the Rockefeller Foundation grant covered initial setup costs, Mercy Corps helped negotiate long-term contracts with large purchasers of recycled goods to stabilize pricing and ensure ongoing profitability of the small franchises.

Throughout this book we have described immersive experiences such as lugging bunches of bananas down the mountain in Zacapa, Guatemala, or journeying on a boat deep into the Amazon to hunt pirarucu with the river communities. These experiences certainly give us interesting stories to share at dinner parties. However, they are also instrumental in our process. By letting people, through their own lives, circumstances, and aspirations tell their stories, we begin to understand their real day-to-day challenges and thus, are able to collectively reframe problems and generate innovative solutions. We illustrate further how this immersive process generates insights with projects in Timor-Leste and Cambodia during which our teams lived and worked alongside frontline communities.

From the Economics of Rice Farming to Education in Timor-Leste

The bag of rice on the ground in the outdoor kitchen of our host family in Bucoli, a small town in Timor-Leste, was labeled in thick, dark blue letters *Product of India*. This fact would have gone unnoticed had we not just arrived on a rice farm where we would be working and staying for the next several days. Our local partner, the international humanitarian organization World Vision, was worried about the staggering poverty of subsistence rice farmers. Our project was aimed at increasing the supply of local products in grocery stores by connecting small farmers to the supermarket retailers in the capital city of Dili. Or so we initially thought. If there was any place that we should be able to find local rice on the island, we imagined it would be on a rice farm.

Timor-Leste is a Portuguese word meaning the eastern end of the island of Timor, which lies in the middle of the large Indonesian archipelago. For hundreds of years, Portugal was the colonial ruler, but after decades of struggle, the people of Timor-Leste gained their independence in 1975, only to be invaded immediately thereafter by their giant neighbor, Indonesia. After another twenty-five years of armed struggle, the one million people of Timor-Leste finally gained independence from Indonesia in 2002, promptly becoming the poorest nation in Southeast Asia. This history of the national self-determination struggle was alive in our conversations with our host family in Bucoli. The grandparents spoke Portuguese, the parents spoke the Indonesian language (Bahasa Indonesia), and the kids all wanted to learn English.[1]

We had spent the previous few days in Dili, meeting with representatives of DiliMart, a national chain of grocery stores. When we went shopping in a DiliMart, most of the products on shelves were imported not only from other Southeast Asian countries but from Portugal. It showed us either the durability and persistence of age-old trading patterns or just how bad the roads were on the island to make Portugal a better option for sourcing food. Our initial hypothesis, that transportation and infrastructure were the primary barriers to local sourcing of produce from the island, was further reinforced by the eight hours it took for us to traverse the 113 kilometers (70 miles) from the capital.

Timor-Leste is a young country. In 2016 the average age of the 1.3 million inhabitants was only sixteen years old. Dili is filled with youthful energy. Squares and parks are filled with teens wearing jeans and backpacks. But around the table over dinner that first night in rural Bucoli, there were no youths in sight. Although the country's average age might have been in the teens, the household compound consisted mostly of children under five and their grandparents.

The absence of any person in the age range of fifteen to fifty became more salient to us the next day, when we woke with the sun, eager to learn about the mechanics of growing rice. We stepped into the muddy paddy and arranged ourselves in a line and learned how to plant the seeds using a string as a guide for spacing. We worked for hours, our backs aching from bending over. We didn't dare complain, because we were working alongside farmers who were decades older than we were, amazed by their ability to endure the backbreaking work. It was only by toiling in the hot sun that we were able to make sense of our observations. The imported food. The unplanted plots of land we had passed on our journey. That night over a dinner of rice and vegetables, we inquired about the age distribution of the neighboring farms. Our hosts shared that after the war for independence, young men and women were eager to move to the city to pursue an education. They were excited to become teachers and government officials, not farmers like their parents and grandparents. This wasn't a problem that could be solved by newly paved roads and negotiated relationships with supermarket chains. Our partners would have to find ways to make farming attractive for the many young men and women in the country.

Reframing the challenge as one of education and social change rather than economics and infrastructure led World Vision to partner with the National University of Timor Leste to develop and then launch a dedicated agri-business curriculum and faculty. Although our team would have preferred to focus on business-building initiatives, the facts on the ground in Bucoli convinced us otherwise. The agri-business education initiative was needed to begin to change long-term societal norms around the value of the family farm.

Missing the Mark in Cambodia

Although dirty boots have always been part of our repertoire, we became convinced of the importance of sharing our philosophy of deep immersion with our partners, bringing them with us into local contexts after several projects yielded less of an impact than we had hoped. As a group activity, putting on our "dirty boots" to explore a problem can't be delegated to an "away" team. It works best as a shared experience that brings together team members from the whole range of partner organizations. One example was our project in rural Cambodia working to improve childhood nutrition. Malnutrition in Cambodia has steadily decreased from the high rates experienced during the civil war and genocide, when from 1975 to 1979 the Khmer Rouge government under Pol Pot slaughtered an estimated two million of its fellow citizens.[2] However, the improvement began to level off in 2005. Today, nearly a third of Cambodian children are significantly underweight, and the country has the highest rate of stunted children in the region.[3] Unclear as to what was driving these statistics, an international NGO asked us to investigate further.

Two weeks immersed in rural village life helped shape our perspectives. Our team attended training sessions where community health workers weighed babies and attempted to convince mothers of the importance of nutrition. We tagged along to NGO-sponsored cooking classes, where carefully selected community members taught mothers how to grow and incorporate more vegetables in their children's diets. We spent days hanging out and experiencing life with a few families as they farmed, shopped for food, and cooked their meals. We were curious whether the lessons from the training were being incorporated into daily life.

It was abundantly clear that the mothers cared deeply about their children's health and wanted them to be strong. They repeated many of the facts learned in the health and nutrition training programs. However, they told us that they simply did not see their children as significantly malnourished. "Our children are not sick or hungry." They have plenty of rice to eat, an abundant and preferred staple of the Cambodian diet. In fact, even when community members showed them evidence that their children were smaller on average than other children around the world, they countered, "But they are the same size as their cousins." When we sat down with several families in the village for hearty meals, we watched as the whole family filled up on rice and broth, feeding the untouched vegetables that had been boiled in the stew to the pigs. We know firsthand the perennial problem of parents getting their children to eat their vegetables, but given the consequences in Cambodia, all that wasted nutrition struck a different chord.

Improving childhood nutrition required more than NGO-sponsored cooking classes. It would require a seismic societal-level shift in both values, which prioritize thinness, and behaviors, to replace rice with a more diverse diet. But those changes take time, which would result in years of irreparable harm to generations of children. Perhaps we could come up with a faster way to improve nutrition in the interim.

Our research pointed us to studies that indicated that fortifying the diets of nursing mothers could have a significant impact on their babies' long-term health outcomes, potentially mitigating some of the stunting. But what to fortify? We noted that this strategy had been executed successfully in the United States, where salt is fortified with iodine.[4] We compared notes from our shopping trips and meals that we prepared with the various families. We noted that the only consistently purchased and utilized item was monosodium glutamate (MSG), a flavor enhancer that is a staple of restaurants and processed foods worldwide. Although no MSG was manufactured in Cambodia, there was a single importer who purchased and packaged it under a number of different brand names. We devised a strategy that involved our NGO partner leveraging their government contacts to lobby that importer to add vitamins to improve the nutritional value of the MSG that families were already purchasing.

We were hopeful that our time spent immersed in village life may have enabled our team to brainstorm a creative solution. We presented our ideas to our partner, excited that we had devised a pragmatic near-term approach that could be effective in reducing malnutrition.

However, their reaction was less than enthusiastic. You would have thought we suggested giving children fortified cigarettes.

What we hadn't realized was that NGO staff had for years preached to families about the harmful effects of MSG. Although MSG has not been definitively linked to any negative health outcomes, the US Food and Drug Administration has had reports of what they call MSG symptom complex: headache, sweating, tingling and numbness in the face, chest pain, nausea, and weakness. Reversing their own massage now and recommending MSG to families was unimaginable.

We argued that they don't have to encourage anyone to buy MSG. People are buying it anyway. Fortifying MSG would just be a way of sneaking needed nutrients into something they are already eating.

Our proposal was summarily dismissed.

We would never know whether the Cambodian MSG processor would have adopted our suggestions and fortified their product with nutrients prior to sale.

In the end, NGO executives suggested we should have included someone on our team with a background in nutrition. Indeed, the project would have benefited from the expertise of nutrition professionals. When we assembled our team, we had included NGO staff with program and education experience, but we overlooked a powerful stakeholder group with a critical perspective. Instead of including them in our problem solving, we presented a solution that posed a threat to their existing values. In hindsight, we should have invited a nutrition specialist from the NGO staff to accompany us to the rural villages, so that they could witness for themselves the constraints on the problem solving. Maybe if we had gotten our boots dirty together, we could have coproduced solution a palatable to all.

Despite our inability to create buy-in for our idea, our experience in Cambodia nonetheless highlights the power of looking at humanitarian problems from a business lens. Our solution to the problem of malnutrition was rooted in our understanding of market mechanisms. It would not have required any change in consumer behavior—people were already voluntarily buying and consuming MSG regularly. And the fact that one importer sold all the MSG in Cambodia made it easier to think of fortifying it with nutrients as we would have to coordinate with only one supplier. This is the power of combining deeply immersive data gathering with a business perspective. It can illuminate pragmatic approaches that would not have been considered. And when you make sure all the right people are involved in the process, you're more likely to succeed.

Guidelines for an Immersive, Inductive Data-Gathering Approach in the Frontlines

Getting your boots dirty in this type of immersive experience may feel awkward to imagine and downright alien to attempt. Yet these activities provide the critical foundation for business problem solving in the frontlines. Getting your boots dirty requires two important skills: learning to open your heart to the experience and being sensitive to avoid perpetuating the historical power dynamics that are a legacy of imperialism and colonization in many parts of the world. Through our experiences, we have developed the following guidelines to help navigate these complexities, enabling us to recognize the common humanity of those with whom we are working.

To begin with, breaking down barriers that prevent interactions at a human level requires reducing power distances. For example, in many meetings around the world we are introduced using our earned title of "Doctor," but in the frontlines, we are simply Viva and Emily. We are fellow moms, daughters, friends, and sisters. We also consciously seek to reduce perceptions of our differences through the ways that we present ourselves. We choose modest clothing, eschewing visible brands. A general rule is never pack more belongings than most of the frontline families you are visiting actually own. Our backpacks are full of notebooks, a couple of short-sleeve and long-sleeve shirts, long trousers, underwear, toiletries, a water bottle, small gifts and enough Clif Bars for seven hundred calories a day for a few days. (We eat everything we are offered and love trying new local dishes, but sometimes the street food does not love us back; hence, the Clif Bars.) If you cannot pack it in a carry-on backpack, you probably do not need it in the frontlines.

We further break down barriers and encourage conversation by doing activities with others when invited—like cooking, walking, playing. We strategically use silence; those we are visiting inevitably fill it with stories or questions if we wait long enough in companionable silence. Furthermore, we advise all our teams that if the conversation turns away from your direct data-gathering topics, because the person you are with is telling you something that is important to them, put aside your interview guide. Embrace the moment. The sharing of one's story is a gift in itself.

Sometimes sharing experiences across culture and language can be daunting. Wherever possible, we learn and use as much of the native language as we are able. We have learned to incorporate translators into our core team to ensure that we get the real stories that people are telling. Sometimes we initially downplay our language abilities during the first days in order to triangulate the stories we hear with the translators' retelling. However, many of our communications don't need language. We have spent days learning and laughing without a language in common or translators. It is amazing how much you can learn with body language, facial expressions, gestures, and an open heart when you are working on a problem together.

We counsel our teams to employ their senses as they are living and working in frontline environments. Even during interviews, we encourage taking notes across four quadrants on a notebook page to capture our questions, the interviewees' responses, our observations, and our feelings. Adopting such a data-gathering approach moves the problem solving from the realm of the intellectual to the practical. Capturing observations on paper while immersing yourself in the moment can be a lot to juggle. When we are able, we work in pairs, one person participating in the conversation and the other taking notes, either in a notebook or sometimes on a small piece of paper that we always keep in our pockets. Every night we sit and write our field notes from those scraps of paper and our memories and discuss them across the team to fill in the gaps. Sharing our experiences in pairs during the day and in teams in the evening also provides us with an important outlet to process our observations. We often find that people can experience the same event and take away very different interpretations. These evening discussions also provide a safety net so that our teammates can help identify and correct our biases and flaws in the narrative.

Our final guideline is to stay long enough to see real life emerge around you. Without a doubt, the arrival of outsiders is an anomaly for many rural families. Often parents will dress their children in their best clothing, combing and parting their hair, frequently licking down a stray curl. This can work against you if you stay only for ceremonial interactions and ask a few formal questions. Eventually, if you are willing to hang out, the kids start getting dirty, people will let their guard down, and the real conversations will begin. You will instinctively know when this happens. It is often after the work day is done, as the sun is setting, or in the spaces in between moments of structured activity. Those in the frontlines will be curious about you, your life, your experiences. Return the compliment. Moreover, even as you try to be respectful of their traditions, remember that your hosts will more than likely make allowances for your inevitable faux pas, given you are an outsider to their ways. The fact that you have traveled great distances to sit at their feet and hear their stories and share your own makes you vulnerable and signals your earnest interest in them. With an open heart and deep engagement, many will respond to that vulnerability and interest by trusting you with their stories.

The Bumpy Road to Success in Colombia

Engineering the immersive experiences that generate novel insights can prove challenging, as was certainly the case on our first project in Colombia, which explored ways that farmers could transition away from coca cultivation toward selling legal crops. We teamed up with two partners, Pontificia Universidad Javeriana, the oldest and most prestigious university in the country, and Colegio de Estudios Superiores de Administración (CESA), its leading business school. We were immediately impressed with the intellectual capital of our partners. For example, Alessandra of Javeriana was trilingual (Spanish, French, and English), held a master's in conflict transformation, and had worked for the Colombian Embassy in the Middle East and on peace-building programs in the former Yugoslavia. Even with all these qualifications, Alessandra only worked as an assistant at Javeriana. Yet, despite the skills and good intentions, our team stumbled early and often.

Since 2000, the Colombian government has embarked on waves of crackdowns on the coca trade, including aerial spraying of chemicals on coca fields and deploying soldiers to manually pull out coca shrubs to undermine production. Despite these major initiatives, coca remains so pervasive in many parts of the countryside that coca paste is sometimes used as currency for transactions instead of the Colombian peso.

The entire extensive cocaine value chain depends on the first step: small-holder farmers growing coca and harvesting the leaves. Our question was, Could we devise a sufficiently attractive path toward legal businesses to encourage *cocaleras* to voluntarily choose this path over continuing to cultivate coca, despite its risks? The hope was that any localized disruption of coca leaf supply could sufficiently throw off the industry value chain so that government initiatives could make gains against the narco-traffickers. Indeed, what we learned from this first foray into Colombia established the initial fact base and invaluable groundwork that our teams relied on during the subsequent five years when we served Heliodora (whom you met in Chapter 1) and other coca-growing communities around the country on launching their agricultural cooperatives and campesino markets.

Our challenges to data gathering began immediately. We suggested that we should target the areas that are best known for coca production, as they needed such a program the most. However, we received immediate pushback, particularly from our CESA teammates. For example, we suggested that we focus on Putumayo, a department (geographical and governance unit like a province or state) covered with dense foliage on the border with Ecuador, that consistently ranks in the top three departments in Colombia for coca cultivation.

"But no one goes to Putumayo. My family says it's dangerous," protested a CESA MBA student.

"And no one cares about Putumayo. It's not a Bogota priority," offered our Javeriana teammate, well versed in Colombian government affairs.

After similar pushback emerged around all of our location suggestions, we realized that our partners were both unfamiliar with and uncomfortable in the more remote frontlines regions of their own country. Despite their commitment to the project objectives, they were unaccustomed to venturing to such places. In fact, once we decided on Putumayo, several CESA teammates pulled out of the project because they were unwilling to travel to Puerto Asis, its capital, because of safety concerns. Some who decided to travel clearly had limited experience with or tolerance for some of the small inconveniences of traveling outside of dense urban areas.

This disconnect from the daily realities of those living and working in Putumayo was transferred to the project itself. For scheduling, we deferred to our Colombian teammates who had insisted that they were well positioned to coordinate our daily data-collection activities. However, their lack of familiarity with the customs and rhythms of rural life was immediately apparent. On our first full day in Putumayo, Alessandra arranged for a minibus to take all thirteen of us to visit a local farm less than a hundred kilometers from Puerto Assis. The bumpy, unpaved roads were clearly unsuitable for such a large vehicle, turning what they expected to be a short drive into a half-day journey. Upon our arrival at the farm, we piled out of the minibus and were greeted by a very surprised farmer who had clearly not expected us. We stood under the enormous canopy of a tropical ceiba tree, and despite our objections, his wife scrambled to rouse the entire village to bring food for our luncheon. We were mortified. Not only had we inconvenienced the whole community with our lack of communication, but we were unable to gather any useful data because of the disruption we caused.

The following day, those of us who had spent significant time in frontline environments took charge of the data-gathering agenda. We broke into six sub-teams of two and three, a much less intrusive number of guests for any given location. We traded the air-conditioned minibus for rusted-out taxis and spread out through the region. We put on our dirty boots and spent time in the local markets, shadowing traders and visiting food processors. On a two-day trip farther into the wilderness, we visited farms run by coca growers and former rebels. Hand in hand with the two-year-old toddler of a former guerrilla commander, we walked their two hectares of cacao plants and yucca fields and toured the tilapia fish ponds they were digging. As we shared a meal, we not only learned about their efforts to establish a cooperative for cacao (for chocolate) as an alternative to coca but we also listened to the former fighters' stories of the war and their hopes for their children. On our way to visit with enterprising young people who were from coca-cultivating families, but were now harvesting wild jungle acai and palmettos to sell to local food processors, our car literally ran into the pickup truck of the mayor of the neighboring town of Puerto Guzman. As our drivers inspected the vehicles for damage, we took this unexpected opportunity to ask the mayor about his challenges and hopes to transform this rural municipality into a center of primary school education and commerce.

If we had not worn dirty boots and listened to the stories, aspirations, and guidance of those farmers currently growing coca and their neighbors, our team would certainly have missed the main breakthrough insight of the effort. Initially, based on our detailed evaluation of harvests, soil, climate, and yields, our economic analysis of alternative crops such as yucca, sugar, fique, and cacao led us to conclude that these crops would not earn even close to the US$3,000 that a hectare of coca can yield per year. Even a hectare of coffee would barely earn that amount. Because we assumed that legal crops needed to earn the same amount per hectare as coca earns for these small-scale farmers to switch, our team naturally began to worry there might be no path away from coca.

But these *cocaleras* themselves redefined the problem for us. They were willing to accept much lower income per hectare from legal crops. Why? The direct quotes tell the story themselves.

"We were not rich, but we were a happy family after all, until the coca war came and destroyed everything,"

"The apparent wealth of coca was merely a mirage. It brought only pain, death, and destruction."

"We don't need as much money as coca. We just don't want anything given to us. We want someone to buy what we are growing."

"We cannot just fill their hearts—we have to fill their pots so they can eat."

"We want to be treated like human beings, and for a long time, no one has done that."

"Coca is easy to grow and gives us money, but how can I continue living like this if the coca war has taken away my children? I refuse to continue living like this."

Without the immersive experience, we would have never been able to see beyond our balance sheet analysis and appreciate the value of participating in Putumayo's lively society, with its church fairs, sporting events, and parades. Cultivating coca forces families to the fringe of society. They distrust their neighbors, given the dangers of the trade. This is a lonely, isolated life. Without dirty boots, we would have missed how their longing to be accepted back into a vibrant community would make the *cocaleras* perceive the opportunity to learn to grow legal crops, particularly if this path presented their families an opportunity to emerge from the shadows.

This insight, based on the aspirations of the *cocaleras* themselves, redefined the problem in three critical ways: first, the end goal was no longer to completely replace the lost coca income. However, because families would lose income until the new crops could be harvested, our second insight was that we would also need to provide short-term loans, which the families could pay back with time. Third, if and when they attempted their exit from coca, a large number of families in a valley would need to exit together. Narco-traffickers would use threats to intimidate families to keep growing coca, protecting their sources of supply. Thugs could show up at the gates of a few farms. However, if most of the families in the region exited coca together, that might just force the criminal elements to seek alternative coca supplies elsewhere. These insights and essential groundwork provided the basis for us to identify a potential pathway out of growing coca toward legitimate farming that we then applied to communities across Colombia.

Getting our boots dirty is arguably one of the most important elements in our approach to data gathering and opportunity assessment in frontline environments. Whether it's the creation of trash recycling franchises in Indonesia, novel ways to reduce malnutrition in the Cambodian countryside, or a path away from coca cultivation toward legal livelihoods in rural Colombia, the key insights that have changed our perspective and driven our solutions have come while we have opened our hearts to a vast number of memorable people and moving experiences in the frontlines.

Immersion in daily life in the frontlines to explore a potential investment opportunity can be an exhilarating experience, as you meet people with vastly different backgrounds and slowly learn more about a previously foreign context. But how do businesses decide when their data-gathering efforts are good enough? Both good in terms of accurately describing the economic and social environment and enough in terms of the objective of well-informed decision making? The next chapter describes how to test your ideas and determine when you have enough information to move forward with a solid plan.

needs. The World Health Organization classifies malnutrition as a significant public health concern in Kiribati. With 33 deaths per 1,000 live births, a baby born on the island faces worse odds of survival than babies born almost anywhere else in the world. Yet, paradoxically, over 40 percent of adults are obese.[2] What could account for these high levels of malnutrition? And how could they be reduced? These were the questions that we set out to investigate in partnership with the humanitarian services of the Church of Jesus Christ of Latter-Day Saints (LDS).

The Pacific islands were among the first areas to be evangelized by the LDS Church. By the 1920s, Mormon missionaries were living and working widely among the people of the South Pacific. They learned the local languages and over time created many of the prominent educational and social institutions across the Pacific, including the leading ones of i-Kiribati society (i-Kiribati is the term for the Kiribati people). Because of more than a century of ongoing engagement, the LDS Church was deeply respected in Kiribati.

As we learned in our work in Cambodia, malnutrition is a very tough problem, rarely with a single root cause. Rather, it is the result of a confluence of complex economic, social, and environmental factors. As such, before we departed for the remote island nation, our team embarked on broad research into its trade patterns, social norms, even geology. We learned that Kiribati's calcareous soil, formed from crushed and decayed shells and bones of sea creatures, lacked the micronutrients like zinc and iron needed to sustain agriculture. For a society heavily reliant on subsistence living, the lack of fresh water and poor soil would surely make farming a constant challenge. We also discovered that the main revenue line item in the Kiribati government budget is the sale of international fishing licenses, which meant foreign trawlers were catching and exporting fish from the surrounding waters.

Isolated from shipping lanes, with associated high transportation costs, importing food would likely be quite expensive relative to the poverty level of the population. Given these initial impressions, perhaps the main driver of malnutrition was lack of access to nutritious food. More specifically, we hypothesized that this lack of access to nutritious foods was due to the lack of suitable land severely limiting locally grown produce. Our team then proceeded to research how other countries with comparably poor soil adopted nutrient-dense crops and innovative techniques to increase nutritional yields.

Much to our surprise, upon arrival in Kiribati, we found a virtual cornucopia of nutritious produce. For example, the grounds of the government of Taiwan's diplomatic mission revealed stunningly lush and well-maintained gardens growing cabbage, pumpkin, peppers, breadfruit, taro, pandanus, coconuts, and many other fruits and vegetables. At the end of each row sat a big, deep, red barrel of organic liquid fertilizer that Taiwanese agricultural experts had tailored to the unique demands of Kiribati's calcareous soil to improve vegetable yields. Further, despite the increase in international fishing offshore, fish stocks remained plentiful in the waters. Local fishermen using traditional methods delivered sufficient protein to family dinner tables. These multiple observations put our early hypothesis in significant doubt.

To disprove our initial hypothesis required two broad sets of data: the demand for calories among the population and the potential supply of locally grown food on the island. We knew in advance the volume of vegetables and fish that would be needed per person to achieve those caloric and nutrition goals and multiplied that against Kiribati's population to determine the annual demand. Once we arrived in Kiribati, we turned our focus to supply. We stumbled on the most productive land, in this case the Taiwanese diplomatic mission gardens, and collected data on the yields of various produce. Given the sophistication of the cultivation approach the Taiwanese agricultural experts had developed, we adjusted that estimate by cutting it in half to make it more realistic for the average i-Kiribati kitchen garden. We then determined the square hectares in Kiribati that might be available for vegetable and protein cultivation. Having multiplied those two variables, we arrived at an estimate of the annual supply. Comparing the annual demand for nutritious food with the potential annual supply, it turned out that the islands had enough land to grow sufficient vegetables and protein to provide nutritious meals for every citizen. There could still be potential obstacles, given property ownership and the need to clear and prepare the land for agriculture, but the Kiribati islands themselves were of sufficient size, when properly cultivated, to provide enough nutrition for the population. This meant that in the long run, Kiribati would not have to import high-priced food to sustain its population. But we could not stop our analysis there. We needed to get our boots dirty and collect more data about what was really happening. Knowing that it is possible to grow food on the island, we needed to figure out how our i-Kiribati and LDS partners could design programs to make it happen.

We went back to the drawing board and immersed ourselves in island life. This meant casting our net broadly to spend time with anyone who might have a perspective on other drivers of malnutrition. We divided up our team to cover more ground, interviewing doctors and nurses in the local hospitals. We talked to street vendors, cooked dinner with families in their homes, and went fishing with the locals. We listened to representatives from government Ministries of Health and Education and spent time with teachers, administrators, and students at the local schools.

Conversations with nurses at the local hospital gave us our first clue as to one of the drivers of malnutrition. One exasperated nurse told us, "When the moms tell us what they feed their child, they say a balanced diet. But when the child vomits at the hospital, the vomit reveals only rice and a little fish." When island families welcomed us into their homes, our team started looking for vegetable gardens on their homesteads and found very few. And when the family gathered to eat, on the menu was mostly rice and a little bit of fish. When we visited the leading school on the island, Moroni High School run by the LDS Church, we observed that two-thirds of the students purchased their lunch from the cafeteria, where the menu was almost exclusively imported, prepackaged instant noodles. There seemed to be enough calories in the diet but not nearly enough nutrients. These additional observations helped us redefine the problem. It seemed that the i-Kiribati did not either understand or prioritize nutritious food. We recalled our experience in Cambodia and did not want to assume that improving the productivity of the land would put vegetables into children's mouths. Our immersive experiences reframed child malnutrition as an education and behavior change challenge: we needed to encourage families to put more nutritious food into their kids' daily diets.

It turned out that, during our time on the island, we had already encountered a number of factors that, when put together, provided pragmatic initial steps toward an emerging solution. More specifically, our initial visit to the Taiwanese diplomatic mission revealed piles of rotting vegetables at the back of their property, as their gardens produced so many more tons of vegetables than the diplomats could consume. The combination of those wasted vegetables and the unhealthy processed noodles served at the high school gave our team an inkling of an idea. Perhaps the LDS Church, which both operated the high school and was well respected in the community, could broker an arrangement with the Taiwanese mission.

In fact, the Taiwanese diplomats were happy to donate their extra produce, and the LDS Church was happy to act as an intermediary, facilitating transportation. The lunch ladies were initially skeptical of the idea. But once they realized that the addition of free, donated vegetables allowed them to use fewer noodles each day, reducing their costs and increasing their profits, they embraced the small amount of extra labor required to prepare the meals. One lunch lady even told us that she was excited because more ingredients enabled her to be more creative in her work, finding delicious new combinations to complement the noodles.

In a short time, the Taiwanese mission was providing truckloads of fresh vegetables to the lunch ladies every week. In effect, given its prominence, the Moroni High School lunches became our demonstration project of the very practical possibilities of improved nutrition on the island. Where Moroni High School led, others in i-Kiribati society would surely follow.

With this success under our belts, we attempted to scale up the nutritious lunch program to other schools across Kiribati's islands. However, the excess bounty of the Taiwanese mission's gardens proved to be a fortunate but anomalous circumstance. The logistics across the archipelago were such that the initial Moroni High School feeding program was sadly not replicable. Our team needed to readjust again.

In the end, together with our LDS partners and a number of other i-Kiribati institutions, our team developed a portfolio of initiatives to attack the child malnutrition problem from multiple angles. We asked the Taiwanese mission to distribute their fertilizer recipe widely and to design gardening and cooking classes for the LDS missionaries to conduct. We even utilized the preferred i-Kiribati communication medium, the radio, to spread the word about nutrition. With the help of the LDS Church, our team organized a nationwide competition to come up with the best short jingles to promote nutrition. Excited students formed teams, and the jingles kept coming in, nearly overwhelming the judges as they sorted through them for days. The winning teams got pride of place to sing their jingles on the national radio.

What each of these initiatives had in common was that their sustainability was based on a conception of self-interest of the participants. We had the proof of concept at Moroni High School—the lunches were both healthy for students and more profitable for the lunch ladies. The Taiwanese mission was only too happy to provide their overabundance of fresh vegetables to the Moroni High School lunch initiative, not to mention their fertilizer recipe free to the public to earn goodwill with both the Kiribati government and its people. The Mormon missionaries enjoyed teaching the cooking and gardening classes. And the kids loved making up jingles if it gave them a chance to be famous for a moment on the national radio. Of course, malnutrition cannot be solved in a day or a week or a month; nonetheless, these initiatives combined to drive momentum toward better nutrition outcomes.

Failing Fast

Our experience in Kiribati demonstrates how working in the frontlines means being willing to have your ideas *fail*. And fail *fast*. This means quickly testing all of our assumptions and working solutions against the data that we gather with our dirty boots, abandoning ideas quickly and changing them if the data do not support them. Failing fast does not mean failure in the traditional sense—with final consequences like a business going bankrupt or a student not graduating from school. Rather, by failing fast we mean not being too attached to your ideas and being open to evidence on the ground even when it indicates that your initial solutions will not work. Confronted with such evidence, you jettison the idea and move on to the next one. Although your initial idea may fail to generate the ultimate solution, embracing this flexible and adaptive mindset means that your problem-solving process will not.

To accomplish this, we use a combination of both inductive and deductive problem-solving frameworks.[3] Chapter 8 discussed our inductive data-gathering method and emphasized how broad, immersive experiences allow us to generate new insights. However, those insights alone cannot drive solutions in the frontlines. They must be combined with a rigorous and rapid way to test those ideas to determine whether they are the product of idiosyncratic experiences or represent a pervasive pattern. In this chapter, we focus on the deductive portion of this framework, which quickly investigates ideas to see whether they are generalizable, viable, and scalable.

The deductive problem-solving process begins with an initial hypothesis, also called a working solution. This doesn't have to wait until you are immersed in the field. In fact, it is useful to enter a new environment armed with a hypothesis developed through background research. In Kiribati, our initial hypothesis was that there was not enough food-growing potential on the island. This hypothesis directed our data collection to disprove that hypothesis by assessing whether the islands could, in fact, grow sufficient nutritious calories for the population. The data we collected, comparing the potential annual supply of nutritious vegetables with the annual demand, indeed disproved that hypothesis. Although one lush garden in the Taiwanese mission could not feed the entire nation, it proved that it is possible to grow fruits and vegetables in large quantities. The country was not doing so—yet. But it could. Our team embraced that dissonance. We actually celebrated when our data disproved our earlier hypothesis. Problem solving in unfamiliar environments requires embracing failure, constantly redeveloping new hypotheses of the solution based on the new data. As Thomas Edison exclaimed, "I have not failed. I've just found 10,000 ways that won't work."[4]

Many hesitate to put forward a hypothesis of a solution so early in the process, as they fear that they know or understand too little about the situation. They perceive early failures as discrediting the process. However, the point of the hypothesis is not to be correct—an almost impossible target right at the beginning. Rather, its purpose is to help organize all subsequent data gathering to prove or disprove the main aspects of the hypothesis. As more data come in, the hypothesis gets modified, transformed, or even thrown out. If it makes you feel better, you can call it a guess. But that initial guess is the key to quickly mobilizing subsequent analytical activities.

Formalizing our hunches into working solutions helps identify the jugular issues. We examine and test these issues first. If the idea fails, then we have disproven it quickly. This points us back to our inductive immersive process to generate a new hypothesis. This iterative process continues as we use data to refine our ideas, cycling through revisions, until such time those newly collected data change the solution less and less. We constantly ask ourselves, "What data would I need to see to disprove this solution?" Another variation of this line of questioning would be to ask, "How wrong could we be?" and "How does that change the answer?" And thus, the hypothesis jump-starts the problem-solving process.

The example in Kiribati also demonstrates the importance of collecting data broadly and returning to observations that may have seemed irrelevant, unimportant, or tangential at the time. Data rarely present themselves in an orderly fashion, and often the key findings appear out of overlooked information. For example, our preliminary research revealed that Kiribati was one of only thirteen remaining countries that had diplomatic relations with Taiwan. This interesting but seemingly inconsequential fact ended up playing a significant role in our recommendations. It helped explain why the Taiwanese mission could devote so many resources to its gardens. With so few missions around the world, there was little competition for funds. Moreover, this gave us confidence for our multiple requests for vegetable donations, their fertilizer formula, and even the design of cooking and gardening classes, as the Taiwanese perceived these initiatives as a way to fulfill their diplomatic mission. Indeed, they were delighted to help.

When we begin any new project in the frontlines, our initial hypothesis will be proven wrong almost all of the time, despite our combined fifty years of problem-solving experience in these environments. The point is not for the first or second or even third hypothesis of the solution to be right. The synthesis of currently available information into a hypothesis helps organize the ensuing data-gathering efforts to prove or disprove that hypothesis quickly and then follow the data to change it accordingly.

From Hammocks to Prison Food in Honduras

The nearly two hundred families of the village Bosques de Santa Lucia is one of Honduras's poorest communities. Like the rest of the country, there are high levels of gang violence, narco-trafficking, corruption, and underemployment. Many of the men have migrated, either to the big cities or to the United States, in search of work, leaving behind less educated older couples and single mothers with multiple children. For a long time, the community survived by selling traditional hand-woven hammocks and other handicrafts in makeshift stands alongside a dangerous highway. Hammocks are an important element of the tropical Honduran culture. As most impoverished homes have but one room, each night the family stretches out and hangs their hammocks in the living room to sleep. Sometimes, they may hang them outside or among the trees to catch the evening breeze. There was certainly demand for hammocks by Honduran customers, and those produced in Bosques de Santa Lucia were stunning—handwoven from local yarn, their colors were as vibrant as the sky, flowers, and hills of the surrounding countryside. The community took great pride in creating the textile patterns. Skilled weavers passed down their secrets to subsequent generations. In 2019, an international humanitarian NGO, Food for the Poor, invited our team to see whether we could commercialize the community's hammocks to bolster the village economy.

However, Honduran customers had a utilitarian view of hammocks—they were needed to sleep in. Cheaper versions were imported from China. Unfortunately, the craftsmanship of the hammocks was unimportant to customers, and thus they were not willing to pay a premium for them. We spent time with community leaders explaining the economics of imported versus locally woven hammocks and how the aspirations of the well-meaning NGO had suggested an economic activity that was neither profitable nor sustainable. Many in the audience were visibly upset at the news, despondent even. Some community members with whom we had worked most closely accused our team of being like all other outsiders—those who promise much and deliver rather less. Disheartened at the news, many local parents shared that they had woven hammocks late into the night, hoping to earn enough income to send their children to the primary school in the next town over, as their own community was too small to sustain a school.

Indeed, this failure did not feel like a routine part of the problem-solving process.

But listening to the worries and honoring the emotions of the community members helped us refocus on the original goal—improving the village economy. Everyone's eye had been on selling more hammocks, but they were just a means to an end. Our objective was to help the community earn enough income to educate their children, not to commercialize hammocks.

We went back to work.

Earlier that week we had noticed, while being given a tour of the area by community leaders, a large building in the distance, surrounded by an enormous wall with barbed wire on the top. We learned that it was a prison, and in fact, this region hosts the largest maximum-security prison in Honduras. We thought, at the time, that the presence of the prison was evidence of how remote this community was from the rest of the country. Our hosts had told us that the government chose the location, far away from densely populated cities, because prison breaks are common in Honduras, and officials wanted to contain the threat to the general citizenry.

Recalling that observation, we wondered whether the proximity of this prison could also be an underutilized asset for the community. Hundreds of families traveled across Honduras, often by bus, every weekend to visit their loved ones in prison. We saw the line forming on Friday, as visitors vied for a chance to enter the compound on Saturday or Sunday. The area surrounding the prison had no infrastructure to support the visitors. We watched them carry all their supplies with them, including food for their incarcerated family members.

We decided to talk to some of the family members waiting in line. We spoke with a grandmother traveling with her two small grandchildren to visit her son, Gabriel, who had been in prison for almost a year. She told us that they had left early Thursday morning and taken several buses to traverse the almost 300 kilometers (185 miles) from their home outside of Tegucigalpa. They brought as little as they could for themselves, saving the scarce space on the crowded bus for necessities for her son—clothes, food, and medicine that would get him through until they were able to visit again in a few months. When they arrived on Thursday night, long after the sun had set, there was already a queue of several dozen families who had arrived before them. Position in line is crucial, because the prison guards restrict access to only a small number of families each Saturday and Sunday morning. It is almost impossible to know how many people would be permitted entry on a given weekend. So it was there that they sat, stood, or squatted, for the next day or two, through the colder nights and the sweltering days, to increase their chance of seeing Gabriel. They snacked on cold fried pupusas they had wrapped in a towel and brought with them. They told us that they wished that they could have a cold drink or a warm meal while they waited.

We wondered, could members of the community make money by providing these visitors with food? This could be both an economic opportunity and a way to ease the burden for people like Gabriel's family.

The community was excited but didn't want to fall into the same trap as the hammocks, so they adopted this idea incrementally. On the very first morning, they set up a roadside stand from which they served horchata drinks and fried meals that sold out by noon. Over time, their cooking grew alongside the demand. Working and saving diligently, the community cautiously invested in other economic prospects associated with the prison. Several families came together to launch a bakery, which became one of the most profitable and highest-employing businesses in the region. Other families focused on producing eggs from their chicken coops or building hydroponic gardens in their backyards to support the burgeoning demand for ingredients. Once the community's success caught the eye of local officials, they tried to demand a fee for the privilege of selling food outside the prison. However, with the support of the local Catholic priest, a local NGO—Cepudo, and staff from Food for the Poor, community leaders were able to meet officials from the ministry for national prisons in Tegucigalpa and obtain an official license to sell food at the prison without having to make any payments to local officials.[5] The community soon began to diversify its offerings by feeding guards and prisoners, and even establishing a roadside restaurant. Families were able to triple their average income and used the extra resources to rent a bus to take their children to the primary school in the next town.

Failing Forward Through Keeping Sight of Core Values

It is not enough to fail fast; those failures must drive toward new and innovative solutions, in other words, you must fail forward. Although we always embraced the value of failing fast, working with our US Special Forces soldiers, we learned the importance of failing forward. One of our soldiers, Jeff, explained it to us this way. On deployment, missions have ends and means. For example, his commander sent his Special Forces team to rural, mountainous Ecuador with the following mission: to seal off the overland narco-trafficking routes between Ecuador and Colombia. His team had full flexibility to choose the means toward these ends. At first, they attempted to stand up a new force, what would have been Ecuador's first counter-narcotics police force, and then train them in small-unit tactics so that they could deploy to this region together. However, this plan met with political controversy due to resistance to creating a new powerful armed force to compete with existing groups. Jeff and his team regrouped to learn from their initial failure. Working with local municipal leaders, they devised a second plan to recruit and train 120 officers from three different existing divisions of the national police and army. This was enough to reduce opposition to the initiative. Execution of this plan became the catalyst needed for Ecuador to have the skills, capabilities, and political commitment to choke off land routes for drug shipments across the Ecuador and Colombian border. The soldiers never compromised on the mission ends, yet they were willing to experiment with almost any means to accomplish them.

What failing forward represents is the importance of clearly articulating and then reminding each other of the overall objectives and core values of the effort. This is particularly important because simply managing the daily operations and logistics of working in frontline environments can be so demanding. In the case of Bosques de Santa Lucia, Honduras, failing forward meant recognizing that our team was not in Honduras to commercialize hammocks—the original question asked of our team—but rather to uplift a community by improving economic outcomes. This wasn't about the traditional patterns and the local yarn. It was about enabling parents to send their children to primary school using a set of skills and assets that they already had. When we were reminded of the broader picture and the motivation of parents, our team was able to identify other options for their community to earn more revenue. These options, including selling meals to prison visitors, inmates, and guards, were consistent with what the community valued most—earning sufficient income to better educate their kids.

Failing forward rests on the firm embrace of these meaningful and well-considered core objectives. When the data inevitably force our team to reconsider potential solutions, we consciously recall the original goal. All options toward that target are on the table and should be considered. That way our process continues to head forward toward the ultimate objective. Failing fast and forward rests on adaptive and flexible systems. It requires trust in the judgment of those living and working in the frontlines. Thereby, each failure in the problem-solving process becomes just another step in progress toward the goal.

Guidelines for Failing Fast and Failing Forward in the Frontlines

We offer several guidelines on how to enable teams to effectively fail fast and forward when problem solving under the extreme levels of uncertainty found in the frontlines. Much research has revealed the biases that each of us face in decision making.[6] More specifically, confirmation bias is the very human tendency to cherry-pick information that confirms our existing beliefs or ideas. As a result, we tend to ignore any information that contradicts those beliefs. Anchoring bias is the tendency to rely too heavily on the first piece of information we receive on a topic. It is the reason that first impressions last. Regardless of the accuracy of that first impression, we use it as a reference point, an anchor, to make subsequent judgments. Without a process in place to force the articulation and rigorous testing of assumptions, it is likely that any problem-solving effort will be subject to those biases.

Furthermore, it is vital that businesses not only go where the data take them but specifically seek out disconfirming data. Being prepared to readjust quickly—to fail fast—gets you closer to a workable solution. Without bringing that humility to learn and change preconceived ideas in the face of conditions on the ground, it really is impossible for businesses to innovate enough, or earn enough trust, to work in the frontlines.

Moreover, human nature leads one to love one's own ideas and hold on to them. Therefore, our teams embrace an obligation to dissent. If any one of us senses something is amiss, like missing data, analytical flaws, overlooked questions, or even mistaken directions, it is their duty to bring it to the team's attention. If any team member gets a sinking feeling regarding the partner, the community, or the problem, we encourage them to honor that feeling and bring it forward to the team. That intuition most likely indicates an as yet neglected issue. Problem solving in frontline environments is constantly a struggle of compounding uncertainties and a serious lack of data. The obligation to dissent helps the team not to forget or lose sight of critical issues.

To reward dissent, our teams embrace a rule of "three points for bad news." Although we often don't actually keep score, we try to encourage dissent by points; any good news gets one point, but any bad news gets three. It is human nature to try to hide or disregard anomalous data that subvert current conventional wisdom. By consciously putting this rule in place, we are turning human nature on its head, incentivizing uncovering data that contradict the current direction of the solution. In the case of our project in Kiribati, it was when two teammates came back from the Taiwanese Mission and exclaimed, "You should see these gardens. They can grow anything!" From this observation, we had to draw a tentative implication that perhaps sufficient nutritious food could be grown on the islands. Or when two other teammates came back from the hospital saying, "We think the nurses believe the mothers do not know how to prepare nutritious meals for their kids." If the mothers thought they were providing nutritious food for their children, but the nurse's observations were to the contrary, then perhaps there might be an education problem. The hypothetical solution to the problem we're trying to solve must adjust to match the emerging data.

Getting Too Excited About a New Opportunity at Women's Textile Cooperative in Palestine

Child's Cup Full (CCF), a textile cooperative in Palestine, hires disadvantaged women, mostly refugees, to produce handmade leather goods. Palestine has a long history of producing high-quality leather goods, and the CCF cooperative (and its brand Darzah), features traditional *tatreez* embroidery, a centuries-old art form that is passed down from mother to daughter. Each shoe or purse is hand-embroidered and celebrates Palestinian cultural heritage.

CCF's founder, Dr. Janette Habashi, is a petite, dark-haired human relations professor with expertise in child trauma at the University of Oklahoma. Janette is also a force of nature. Born and raised in Palestine, she describes herself as anti-capitalist and anti-imperialist. But do not let that philosophy fool you, as she is a shrewd businesswoman who has built CCF's operations from the ground up. In 2015, when nearly two-thirds of young women in the West Bank were unemployed, Janette recruited our team to develop strategies to scale up the operations to provide more economic opportunities for the equal numbers of Muslim and Christian Palestinian women she hires for the workshop. As she launched our joint effort, she proclaimed, "We do not hire women to make shoes. We make shoes to hire women."

The West Bank is small, about the size of the state of Delaware. Yet the current political and governance arrangements make the supply chain to assemble leather shoes incredibly lengthy and complex. The Darzah center, where the women design and embroider the shoes is in the north, in Zababdeh. The traditional center for leatherworking was in Bethlehem, in the south. The leather cuttings must traverse the West Bank back and forth between Zababdeh and Bethlehem several times before the shoes are complete. Navigating the multiple Israeli military checkpoints on the 120-kilometer (75-mile) highway between the two workshops could sometimes take a full day. Our team identified this as a pain point in the supply chain and hypothesized that one way to scale up would be for CCF to bring all of the leatherworking steps into their own operations.

The women artisans in Zababdeh very quickly got excited about this prospect. There was no small amount of pride at the possibility of women making the shoes from beginning to end. Moreover, they had long suspected that the leather workers in Bethlehem, almost exclusively men, were overcharging them for their services. Janette loved the potential marketing story of fashionable shoes sold in New York City that were entirely designed, embroidered, and manufactured by empowered Palestinian women. Janette's sister, Georgette, who was responsible for all of the transportation, could not wait to jettison her daily logistics and security checkpoint nightmares. Our confirmation and anchoring biases almost got the best of us as momentum built toward this initiative.

We mapped each step of the industry value chain, including costs and revenues, from early designs to raw material purchases to cutting the soles, through to the final assembly of the shoes and boots. The data surprised all of us. First, the leatherworking steps controlled by the artisans in Bethlehem were not as lucrative as we expected. Furthermore, to bring this step into their own operations in Zababdeh, the cooperative would need to purchase specialized equipment, including an industrial laser cutter and heavy-duty sewing machines, not to mention pay for the advanced training to use them. Comparing the sizable upfront investment costs of expensive equipment and training with the more modest increase in margin by manufacturing the entire shoe, the cooperative would not pay back the investment in a reasonable time. Within its current operations, control of the entire shoe production value chain by bringing the leather working steps in-house would not increase the cooperative's profits. Once again, we had failed. But how could we fail forward?

Our team stepped back to reflect on Janette's original vision. In this case, failing forward meant recognizing that we were not in Palestine to redesign the leather shoe value chain but rather to build business opportunities so that CCF could hire more women, thereby improving the daily lives of those still living in refugee camps in the West Bank. This wasn't about the traditional Palestinian patterns and the fine quality local leather. It was about uplifting disadvantaged women using their existing skills. Ultimately, where our team could support CCF was to develop a sales plan to approach big wholesale and retail apparel customers in the United States to negotiate large seasonal purchase orders for Darzah's new shoes. A prominent American retailer ended up making a large order.

To fulfill the order Janette hired several dozen women. However, it was almost impossible to accommodate this new workforce at the Zababdeh workshop. Ironically, rather than aggregating this work in a single location as we had originally hypothesized, Janette ended up going in the opposite direction—disaggregating the operations. Instead of hiring more workers to come to the workshop, Janette devised a system by which CCF could hire many more women part time in nearby communities to make the embroidery for the shoes. Many traditional Muslim households would not permit their women to work outside the home. By bringing the materials to them and picking up the finished product, CCF could enable these women to work in their own homes, for a few hours a day, and earn their own money. As a bonus, Georgette's logistics challenges were simplified; instead of the uncertainty of trying to cross the checkpoint multiple times in a single day as a Palestinian woman, she was able to collect all the embroidery from homes in neighboring villages and only had to cross the north-south military checkpoints once a week to transport the embroidery and cut leather materials to the Bethlehem factory to sew the finished shoes.

This deductive problem-solving framework allows us to quickly test the viability and scalability of working solutions to access opportunities in frontline environments. At the heart of the process is taking what data you have and synthesizing it into a hypothesis of the solution and using that hypothesis to organize all subsequent data gathering efficiently and effectively to prove or disprove it. Follow the data to change your ideas until incoming data change the solution in incrementally smaller ways. Whether it is selling handmade hammocks in Honduras or shoes entirely handmade by Palestinian women, do not be afraid of being wrong. Assume you will be wrong and celebrate it. Fail fast, gathering data quickly to disprove a proposed solution, and fail forward, always keeping sight of the ultimate goal.

These chapters have shown that there is money to be made out there in the frontlines, and those with the vision and the guts to move first will turn their efforts into profit. Yet how will business impact the societies they plan to expand into? The potential benefits to society mirror the benefits to business. The final chapter turns its attention to the many varied ways business will impact, through its investments and operations, the world's toughest places.

CONCLUSION

Nothing Stops a Bullet like a Job

Society and business both benefit from working in frontline envi-
ronments.

Our friend Wayne Murdy from Newmont Mining has a saying. Any
investment that he undertakes must have two things. First, there
must be a solid business case. Second, there must be an upside, or some
intangible benefit that makes a deal feel like it might become a home
run—be it the potential to open future markets, reinforce the organization's unique culture, or provide a significant additional advantage that
is hard to quantify.

We have spent the previous nine chapters demonstrating that business can thrive and improve lives in some of the world's toughest places.
The frontlines represent vast, rapidly growing, and underdeveloped
economic potential. As estimates of annual economic activity in frontline environments approach nearly $20 trillion (at purchasing-power

parity), clearly, this is a lucrative overlooked opportunity. The unrelenting logic of growth demanded by shareholders inevitably requires businesses to seek opportunities in increasingly unstable regions. Adopting a stripped-down business model, cultivating multiple local partnerships, and implementing a disciplined approach can help businesses address the complexity and instability of the frontlines. Businesses will need to embrace a long-term view, new skills, a little humility, and ongoing troubleshooting to be successful. Our field-tested process helps you understand and navigate opportunity while managing the costs and risks inherent in such an expansion. We have also argued a case for a reasonable upside—that business can enhance existing development and security initiatives and improve lives by providing the dignity of work for families and communities.

Over the years we have discussed our ideas with business executives, government officials, NGO staff, and military officers. Many have already embraced our approach and incorporated our process into their organizations. However, a small chorus of senior business leaders of large multinationals have pushed back. One senior partner at a prominent professional service firm told us that his hesitation was not due to lack of confidence in the size of the opportunity but rather based in fear of the unknown: "Nontraditional competition from men with guns scares me more" than the potential benefit.

This reticence made us reevaluate whether we had accurately assessed either the business case or the upside. We are confident in the business model, as we have seen it generate returns repeatedly around the globe. The overall size and attractiveness of the frontlines opportunity combined with the threat of competitors gaining a first-mover advantage should motivate the next round of globalization and investment in the frontlines. However, these questions made us reflect upon whether we had accurately described the benefits that accrue to individuals, communities, and society in general.

So let us make the case for the upside. Because business is so fundamental to all societies, our approach has the potential to change society on a grand scale, both abroad and at home. If transforming individual lives and communities through work is not a sufficient upside, business needs to work in the frontlines because it represents the scaffolding that other critical relationships can be built upon, so that societies can not just survive but thrive.

Upside: J&J and the Capacity to Solve Grand Challenges

In the summer of 2020, BOTFL alum Christopher Villani had just landed the biggest job of his decade-long career at Johnson & Johnson (J&J). He was promoted to be the market director in charge of planning their COVID vaccine rollout in the United States. Even before he interviewed for the position, Chris had reached out to us for advice as to how he might approach the challenge. Although his tone was upbeat, you could hear the stress in his voice. "Well, we're not in Kansas anymore," he said, clearly feeling the pressure of his potential role and the uncharted territory he would be facing.

Developing vaccines during the global COVID-19 pandemic required decisions to be made under tremendous uncertainty. Pharmaceutical companies had to innovate under pressure to produce the most effective vaccine as quickly as possible and simultaneously navigate the many different national regulatory bodies, each with different criteria and processes for approval. This alone was a Herculean feat, but Chris knew that there was an even bigger challenge ahead—figuring how to get the approved vaccine into the arms of every adult around the world.

J&J leaders immediately decided that if they were to accept the challenge of creating a COVID vaccine, it would be what they called "the people's vaccine." It would have to be not only safe and effective but affordable, transportable, and easy to administer so that it was accessible to all—both home and abroad. They looked to the company's value statement to guide this strategy: "We believe it is our responsibility to protect people, especially the most vulnerable, from the world's most challenging and wide-reaching infectious diseases."[1] Their vaccine differed from other early movers in that it did not require specialized, ultracold refrigeration. In fact, theirs was the only early vaccine that could be stored in a regular fridge. They knew that speed to protection was paramount and compliance to second doses of vaccines would be low, so they were the only company to study their vaccine in a single-dose trial. It had the advantage of being the only single-dose vaccine that did not need specialized refrigeration during the pandemic. J&J also developed a straightforward pricing strategy during the active phase of the pandemic, charging US$10 per dose to facilitate access around the world and speed of implementation. It was approved in 113 countries, covering much of southeast Asia and all of Africa and the Caribbean.[2] More than one hundred million doses of the J&J vaccine were administered in the first wave of vaccinations, making up 10 percent US shots during that period.[3] It became the vaccine of choice to administer to vulnerable populations like those in poor neighborhoods, rural communities, and those experiencing homelessness.[4] It allowed for pop-up vaccination sites to serve migrant workers and the working poor who often live in close quarters. Public health officials lauded J&J's vaccine, calling it an important tool in fighting the spread of COVID-19.[5]

Chris and his team were responsible for planning the J&J vaccine rollout in the United States. The traditional tried-and-true approach in product rollout would not work here. In nonemergency situations, pharmaceutical companies, armed with years of evidence from clinical trials regarding the safety and efficacy of new medications, largely target their marketing and awareness efforts at physicians, emphasizing the drug's technical features and benefits. They also facilitate product distribution by negotiating with payers such as insurance companies and government programs such as Medicare who will foot the bill. The early stages of new drug launches focus on driving awareness through prioritizing early adopters and major prescribers, who mainly practice in large academic medical centers. However, in this case, awareness wasn't the problem. The entire world sat at home, glued to their televisions, waiting for news of a breakthrough. The key challenge was speed. How could J&J quickly increase the number of people vaccinated?

Creating a vaccine that could be delivered easily and affordably was a critical first step but was not sufficient. Effective pandemic management required changing the hearts and minds of many individuals hesitant to get vaccinated.

"How do we build trust quickly?" Chris posed the question to us. "This feels like classic BOTFL," he continued. "We need to approach this as if we were one of our teams making recommendations in the field!"

Chris's team realized that there was a portion of the population who were skeptical of the speed with which the COVID vaccines were developed. To reach those people, it was necessary to demonstrate the efficacy of the science around vaccines development. In this case, this meant emphasizing educational initiatives that would support overall vaccination levels, not only the adoption of a particular type of vaccine. Typical business metrics of share, preference, and product volume were trumped by overall vaccination rate and trust in vaccines. By avoiding competitive messaging around the virtues of its own vaccine and instead emphasizing what was commonly true among the available vaccines, J&J prioritized generating overall trust in vaccinations rather than attempting to shape physician or consumer brand preferences, which would have slowed vaccine uptake and ultimately cost lives.

Building trust was also essential among populations whose historical interactions with the government-mandated health-care system was fraught with misgivings and mistrust. Indeed, those populations most likely to be skeptical of both the vaccines and the government were also those most negatively impacted by the virus itself. The result was that those most overrepresented in COVID deaths—namely, African Americans, Latinos, and rural communities—were the least likely to receive the vaccine. Much of this distrust was warranted, particularly in the African American community, where there was a history of exploitation. For example, many recall the decades-long Tuskegee Study of Untreated Syphilis in the Negro Male experiment conducted by the US Public Health Service that withheld treatment from four hundred Black men in Alabama to understand how syphilis presented as the disease progressed.[6] As a result, many poor and historically marginalized groups are distrustful of the medical establishment and reluctant to adopt public health measures such as drug interventions and vaccinations.[7] These skeptical groups needed to receive the information about the COVID vaccine from sources they already trusted.

Embracing the lessons learned from his BOTFL experience, Chris and his team mapped the landscape of influential institutions, organizations, and individuals. They actively sought common ground with organizations that a pharmaceutical company would not normally engage with and designed a communication plan that depended on partnering broadly. J&J turned to Black churches who represented the most trusted institution in troubled times. Chris and his team mobilized outreach with faith leaders whose endorsement would likely resonate with community members and who had a vested interest not only in keeping members of their congregations safe and healthy but also in enabling in-person gatherings. Pastors and pharmacists partnered at the pulpit to encourage those in the pews to get vaccinated. Black churches also assisted with access, hosting vaccination centers run by area hospitals. Uber and Lyft provided free rides to these church-sponsored vaccination sites. Black churches became "an indispensable partner" to cultivating acceptance of COVID vaccination in African American communities.

Rural America harbored similar skepticism toward the COVID vaccine. Many believed that their more isolated circumstances protected them from infection. Political and ideological differences between rural and urban populations further reduced confidence in the safety of the vaccines. This made rural populations less likely to see the risk-return benefit in getting the new vaccine. J&J turned to the American Farm Bureau, one of the most trusted institutions in the West and Midwest. As a founding member of the COVID-19 Community Corps, the American Farm Bureau and its leaders worked tirelessly to promote informed decisions regarding the vaccine.[8] The Farm Bureau became the backbone of a network of trusted messengers about the vaccine in rural areas. Region by region, community by community, Chris and his team further brainstormed who might be the most respected voices in each context. In the American South, revered college football coaches in the Southeastern Conference (SEC) partnered on COVID vaccine awareness campaigns. Indeed, all of these organizations had an interest to getting back to business as usual.

In the face of this massive public health emergency, when stopping a highly contagious and deadly virus depended on delivering a new vaccine widely to skeptical and vulnerable populations, experience working in the frontlines made a difference. Although the health-care system in the United States is not a classic frontline environment, the conditions of the global pandemic made it resemble the frontlines in its ambiguity and massive uncertainty. Chris and his team employed every element of our process, the same skill set learned through working in typical frontline contexts, to develop the COVID vaccine launch plan. They mapped the entire value chain from citizens obtaining credible information about the vaccines all the way through to traveling to the vaccination appointment on time. They brought deep pragmatism and a fresh eye to the challenge, by instinctively asking which organizations might share common objectives with J&J. They methodically analyzed the landscape of influence of potential nontraditional partners, engaging broadly across society and seeking common ground. They were not afraid to try unconventional strategies, knowing some might not work as expected. They combined both an inductive data-gathering method to generate innovative ideas regarding the vaccine rollout and the deductive problem-solving framework to put them to the test, quickly jettisoning those ideas that would not support the cause of rapid widespread adoption of the vaccine. By embracing the lessons learned from his BOTFL experience and adopting this approach, Chris and his team at J&J devised a rollout program that helped to systematically dismantle the major barriers to quickly drive widespread COVID vaccination. That is the upside.

Upside: Jobs Instead of Bullets

After the Arab Spring swept through the societies of North Africa and the Middle East in 2011, Tunisia was the last country in the region that combined a majority-Muslim population with a functioning democ-racy. Although it had been a relative oasis of stability in the region, threatening clouds were circling Tunisian society. In the five years since it gained global prominence in 2014, the powerful terrorist group called the Islamic State (ISIS) had recruited between three thousand and six thousand Tunisians to its cause, by far the highest per capita recruit-ment rate of any nation.

The militant group had crippled the Tunisian economy through two targeted high-profile acts of terrorism. First, on March 18, 2015, three terrorists attacked tourists on the steps of the world-renowned Bardo National Museum in Tunis, killing twenty-two people. Three months later, a gunman claimed by Islamic State opened fire on a beach on the Mediterranean Sea, killing thirty-eight tourists sunning themselves at the popular resort of Port El Kantaoui. Suddenly, more than one million tourists canceled their vacations to Tunisia, throwing hundreds of thou-sands of young people out of work as the hospitality industry collapsed. This particularly high unemployment and associated hopelessness turns out to be a powerful terrorist recruiting tool. Without the hope of a bet-ter life, isolated young men frequently are enticed by ISIS's promises of belonging to a cause that gives them a sense of purpose and identity. By the time this better life fails to materialize, it is often too late.

In light of this context, the high unemployment rates took on a new urgency. In 2019, we launched a multiyear partnership with local entre-preneurs to improve the economic conditions for growth in Tunisia. Our project focused on finding ways to deliver electricity to industrial man-ufacturers at a lower cost than currently available from the government monopoly. Using solar and wind energy and adopting an innovative business model, large manufacturers of ceramics and electronics, which depend on massive amounts of power, were able to lower their electricity costs by as much as 30 percent. This significant improvement in their cost structure enabled them to expand production, mainly for export to the European Union. This was a compelling business case on its own.

However, the upside for society is almost unquantifiable. Reducing energy costs to expand manufacturing operations wasn't just about reducing unemployment. This was about providing a viable alternative for many susceptible young Tunisians to ISIS's seductive recruitment. As Father Greg Boyle, a longtime friend and the founder of Homeboy Industries, a gang rehabilitation and reentry program in Los Angeles says, "Nothing stops a bullet like a job."

Upside: Reknitting the Social Fabric

The volcanic peaks of the southern island of Mindanao in the Philippines rise above the low-lying clouds and lush green forest. While working on an agricultural value chain project with our Filipino peace-building partner, our team got to observe these majestic peaks from a lot closer than we expected, as we were evacuated from Cotabato City to higher ground because of a tsunami warning of massive flooding along the coastline. Long ignored by the government in Manila, Mindanao possesses all the outward symptoms of neglect—roads pocked with potholes, houses with thatched roofs, and spotty cell phone coverage. In the most recent iteration of ongoing conflict on the island, for almost half a century, Mindanao was engulfed in a violent insurgency that pitted the Muslim Moro population against the national government in a bid for independence. Like many anti-government insurgent forces, they used guerilla tactics, such as bombings, assassinations, kidnappings, and extortion to support their operations. The long insurgency caused enormous suffering, killing more than 150,000 civilians and forcing another 2 million to flee their homes. When the insurgency formally ended in 2014, the negotiated terms of the comprehensive peace agreement dictated that more than twenty thousand former insurgents would disarm and then would be permitted to return to their villages in the newly created Bangsamoro Autonomous Region of Muslim Mindanao.[9]

When the Filipino government and Moro leaders negotiated the locations of the disarmament zones, they mostly considered the safety of the former insurgents once they gave up their weapons. This was particularly important as there was no love lost between the former Muslim guerrillas and their future Filipino Catholic and Indigenous Lumad neighbors who had suffered the effects of the armed conflict for many decades. The ex-fighters were so fearful of reprisals that they agreed to settle only in villages very familiar to them, places where they could melt back into the jungle should they feel threatened. Negotiators on both sides had not given much thought to the challenges of building sustainable and legitimate livelihoods for them. Fortunately, Abu Ebrahim had.

A former Moro commander, Abu Ebrahim returned to his native Maguindanao province in the new autonomous region, bringing with him a detachment of demobilizing insurgents. Despite the peace agreement, the area was still under martial law. There was continued fighting with many groups vying for power including Moro dissident insurgents, Islamic extremists, Communist rebels, rival clans, drug warlords, and roving bandits. When we first met Abu Ebrahim in 2015, he was fit and intense after years of command, although his hair was already prematurely graying at the temples. As befits a military man, he faced his new responsibilities with caution and discipline. He told us that for lasting peace to flourish in this valley, his comrades in arms needed hope for a better future for themselves and their families. Having left home as a teenager to join the insurgency, his education was limited, and he wasn't sure how to deliver this new life to his fellow fighters.

Yet the Maguindanao province possesses a true competitive advantage. The generations of conflict prevented development, leaving much of the natural environment in Maguindanao pristine. Its mountain valleys possess the altitude, soil, and climate ideal for growing high-quality Arabica coffee. Indeed, more than a century earlier, the Philippines were the fourth-largest exporter of coffee in the world. However, the combination of the coffee rust disease epidemic in the late nineteenth century, the volatility in commodity prices and markets in the twentieth century, and the rampant insurgency since the 1970s made coffee production in Mindanao all but collapse.[10] Abu Ebrahim and his fellow demobilized insurgents, nevertheless, could see that their region had the building blocks needed for a viable coffee business.

Many of their family farms still possessed ten- to thirty-year-old coffee shrubs growing in the wild. However, having lost generations of farming knowledge, their initial harvest attempts failed. For example, not knowing any better, Abu Ebrahim and other coffee farmers picked all of the coffee cherries at once, both the ripe dark-red ones and the unripe green ones. They left their coffee cherries on the ground to dry, further diminishing their quality.

A local municipal official introduced Abu Ebrahim to the employees of a Canadian company, Rocky Mountain Coffee, which had operations a few valleys over. Indeed, this company had spotted a market opportunity. The Philippines imports 90 percent of the coffee it drinks. As the economy continues to grow, domestic coffee demand is booming, with a 20 percent annual growth rate. Rocky Mountain Coffee reasoned that, to thrive, Mindanao coffee did not need to immediately reach international quality standards. It just needed to be good enough to be roasted, distributed, and sold to domestic consumers. They saw so much value in the market that they launched their operations in 2004, despite the ongoing conflict. In a business model remarkably similar to that of Green Mountain Coffee, yet at a smaller scale, Rocky Mountain Coffee provides ongoing technical support, training, and management assistance to local small producers, mainly through partnerships and purchase agreements with local cooperatives.

As Abu Ebrahim started to organize his fellow demobilized-insurgents-turned-coffee-farmers into a cooperative, he also sought out his enterprising cousin working in the Middle East, who was able to secure a small amount of seed capital from his boss, a Gulf sheikh. With this money, Abu Ebrahim invested in basic equipment for the pulping, hulling, and drying of coffee beans. His cooperative hired local laborers to do the tedious process of sorting good beans from defective ones. They built raised platforms on which to dry their coffee off the ground. They sold their first harvest to Rocky Mountain Coffee with great fanfare.

In the same way that expanding manufacturing in Tunisia undermined terrorist recruitment, the cooperative in Maguindanao helped keep the hope of peace alive by giving former insurgents an alternative to returning to combatant life. However, although necessary, jobs alone are rarely sufficient to entice anyone to abandon a life of crime and violence. When it comes to pure economics, crime often pays. And in frontline economies, the disparity between what can be made through illegal activity and through legitimate employment is amplified. Without social and economic incentives together, the risk of re-recruitment of young men into armies or militias or criminal activity is high.

Abu Ebrahim told us that for lasting peace to flourish in this valley, his former fighters needed more than just a job; they needed hope for a better future for their families. Even Father Boyle recognizes that "nothing stops a bullet quite like a job" is only part of the story—without the chance to "re-identify who you are in the world," it is easy to slip back into old patterns. That is why his organization, Homeboys Industries, offers not only jobs but tattoo removal for those seeking to escape gang life and turn to the next chapter of their lives. In Maguindanao, the coffee equipment that Abu Ebrahim purchased ended up becoming the foundation that would ultimately foster the beginnings of a tentative peace between his Moro people and his Filipino Catholic neighbors. Business did not just offer an income; it was a practical way to begin to reweave the fabric of society.

By 2018, Abu Ebrahim's coffee cooperative was surviving if not yet thriving. It needed more coffee than the several hundred farms could produce, as coffee processing requires economies of scale to make efficient use of their newly purchased equipment. The combination of geography, demography, and scale economies conspired to contribute a solution, but not one that would come naturally to the Moro community. As we ourselves observed during our unexpected flight from the tsunami, Muslim Moro and Filipino Catholic farming communities sometimes live right next to each other, on different sides of the same mountain valley. After much consultation among his Moro community to build consensus, Abu Ebrahim invited a group of Filipino Catholic coffee farmers living in the same valley into their cooperative. When we asked him why he and his fellow Moros had made this decision, we expected a response encompassing efficiencies, utilization, and reduction of per unit costs. He just shook his head slowly and replied, "Because we are all children of Abraham."

Although wary, the neighboring Filipino Catholic coffee farmers embraced the gesture, and a fragile trust began to build between the two groups. Indeed, these farmers had no other way to process their coffee beans. Their alternative was to sell to middlemen at very low prices. In the end, perhaps thirty Catholic families from the surrounding area joined the cooperative; some even began to work alongside their former adversaries in administering it. After several years of laboring together to make the cooperative a success, you can sometimes see Muslim and Catholic coffee farmers breaking bread together—a sight completely unheard of even five years earlier.

In 2020, Abu Ebrahim proudly pointed out how much life had changed in his village, such as the new construction of modest homes with indoor bathrooms and kitchens. Abu Ebrahim is the first to admit his coffee cooperative did not achieve such business success on its own and credits several collaborations in achieving these outcomes. In particular, the employees of Rocky Mountain Coffee accompanied them each step of the way and provided advice on how to overcome obstacles to their growth. With this assistance, the cooperative was able to register as a formal legal entity. Recognizing the growing complexity of the organization and his limited business experience, Abu Ebrahim stepped down from his leadership role and was replaced by a Filipino Catholic neighbor with managerial experience. He still comes to work every day, continues to be an active member of the cooperative, and provides guidance to the community as needed.

The growth of the cooperative would be a success story in any impoverished rural area. The transformation of former insurgents operating in the informal economy into owner-employees of a formal, incorporated, tax-paying entity with sales contracts with a Canadian company is a compelling example of success. But more importantly, this story demonstrates business's unparalleled ability to bring together for a common cause the most unlikely of partners, in this case those from different sides of a religious divide, in the shadow of a generations-long insurgency. Yet, through initial cautious interactions, ongoing cooperative operations, repeated buying and selling transactions, and conversations that surrounded the business, both sides took small risks to get to know each other better. This process gradually built the trust that grew into active collaboration toward their common business objectives. After such a long and brutal conflict, what has been accomplished in Maguindanao in terms of reconciliation across societal and religious divisions in only five years is nothing short of remarkable.

The story of Maguindanao is not just an example of a path forward to peace and stability in frontline contexts—it is an example that highlights the important role of business in shaping that path.

Upside: Business Provides the Scaffolding on Which Thriving Societies are Built

Whether it is a society torn apart by war, rebuilding after a crisis, or fragmented by political strife, business is uniquely positioned to enable the critical relationships and social cohesion needed for a society to build resilience and, ultimately, to not merely survive but thrive. When two parties interact repeatedly, as is often the case in business transactions, they develop assets that are specific to that relationship, including information about one another, agreement on how interactions should unfold, and sometimes the expectation of reciprocity. This is what social scientists call social capital, and it not only exists in dyadic relationships but as a system of interwoven interpersonal relationships in a society that "facilitate[s] coordination and cooperation for mutual benefits."[11] Dense networks, like kinship in a family or close-knit relationships in small towns, contain high levels of trust, where, feeling a sense of moral obligation, family members and neighbors expect to look after each other. When conflict destroys trust and social capital in societies, interactions become riskier, and individuals limit their interactions to those they trust the most, reducing contact among nonkin neighbors. As the pattern of interaction across a society contracts, it erodes any social ties across different communities, fragmenting a society further, reducing trust and laying the groundwork for continued cycles of recurrent conflict.

Business activity provides a low-stakes way for opposing and diverse groups to interact. These interactions, which are transactional and governed by self-interest, nonetheless can foster the initial seeds of social capital and cohesion. For example, despite being members of opposing political beliefs or religions or tribes or ethnic groups, a buyer and seller coming together to exchange money for goods may eventually learn that they are both parents of young children and thus share a common hope for better education and future opportunities for the next generation. Identifying this common cause can be the beginning of building trust that will eventually lead to social capital. It might prompt a buyer to get their goods or service from that seller, or it might cause the buyer to recommend that seller to others. Over time, this set of interactions expands connections among groups who were previously unconnected.

These transactions alone are not sufficient to build a network of connections that can transcend historical divisions. However, they do provide a reliable channel through which trust-building interactions can occur. When Abu Ebrahim built the consensus among his community to invite Filipino Catholic coffee farmers into the cooperative, he overcame decades of distrust between the two communities. The invitation encompassed not only smart business decision making but also included the well-being of all the residents in the region, ultimately engendering a new level of trust among those residing in Maguind-anao. By tying together the economic fates of the returning insurgents and their neighbors, he not only made a sound long-term business decision, but he also fostered the beginnings of a network of social capital. Through the creation of opportunities as attractive as those represented by the Maguindanao cooperative, even those on the fringes of society may gradually decide to join into the economic activity. As social bonds strengthen and reliable relationships are established, members of a society can use this network to achieve new and unrelated common ends. This increased social cohesion is essential for further economic growth and opportunity. This is the upside as well.

Thus, in addition to the benefits that accrue *to* business from operating in places like Mindanao, and to the individuals participating in the cooperative, further benefits accrue to society more generally *because* business operates in these environments. Business contributes the necessary ingredients to build stability after violence. It provides jobs and a hopeful vision for the future, particularly for young idle men—like in Tunisia and the Philippines—that might otherwise be swept up into violence. Business also provides the platform for the repeated interactions needed to begin to build relationships after conflict. Finally, business also buys society time. It takes time for genuine reconciliation to repair the cleavages in society's fabric. It also simply takes time for individuals to transform their identities from what was to what will be—for example, from guerilla fighter to businessperson. This process can't be hurried. It can understandably take years for communities to accept former combatants as anything other than a threat, and the process is most effective if it is allowed to unfold naturally.

Although NGOs or charities might be invested in achieving reconciliation, the challenge is that philanthropic money always runs out.

Because business is designed to be sustainable and self-propelling, if it is profitable, it represents a preferable option to foreign charity or aid. Profitable business will persist into perpetuity and thus, can provide the time required for the process of reconciliation to unfold.

A Call for Moral Imagination

Even though it has traditionally been left out of the peace-building and development puzzle, business can, when done in thoughtful and careful partnership with other sectors of society, become an integral part of developing solutions for the world's toughest problems. The upsides for both business and society in the frontlines are clear. But these opportunities will not appear organically—leaders must find the courage to recognize and engineer them. This requires what scholar John Paul Lederlach calls "moral imagination," where individuals can transcend the destructive patterns of conflict and recognize turning points and possibilities that pave the way for constructive change. Lederlach argues that these turning points often occur when an individual can see how they are connected in a web of relationships, even with their former adversaries or competition. Abu Ebrahim's moral imagination enabled him to perceive his former enemies as part of his sphere of influence. He was able to imagine an answer to Lederlach's question, "How do we transcend the cycles of violence that bewitch our human community while still living in them?"[12]

Moreover, business leaders with the capacity for moral imagination are in a perfect position to extend the first hand in partnership. And we have encountered a number of such leaders who instinctively grasp this extraordinary possibility. Wayne Murdy, the retired CEO of Newmont Mining, based his company's investment decisions to develop new multibillion-dollar gold mines not only on the solid business case for his shareholders but also on the upside for the communities in which Newmont's mines were embedded. The frontline communities benefited from Newmont's long-term commitment to hiring and training local labor, building up local suppliers, and caring for the local environment. Newmont benefited from access to underdeveloped reserves of valuable minerals in frontline environments. Similarly, the founder of the Palestinian textile cooperative Dr. Janette Habashi did so by consciously hiring an equal number of Palestinian women from historically rival Muslim and Christian backgrounds. And Heliadora, the Colombian *cocalera*, created a new life for herself and her children not only through the arduous work of growing legal crops on her tiny farm but also by reconciling with her neighbors who had perhaps judged her most harshly for cultivating coca. Business leaders with moral imagination, like Wayne Murdy, Dr. Janette Habashi, Heliodora, and Abu Ebrahim, can begin to build resilience in their societies.

Our times are dominated by increasing income disparity, acrimony between polarized parts of society, and escalating criticism of capitalism and business. Yet here we present our rather more optimistic message that all frontlines have opportunities for growth and that pragmatic, disciplined collaboration among nontraditional allies can overcome the barriers to those opportunities. Moreover, our work demonstrates that business plays a crucial and invaluable role in generating solutions to the grand challenges of our time. Whether it is fighting the next contagious disease, rebuilding after war, eliminating poverty, or fighting the exploitation of vulnerable children, business provides a set of disciplined principles and processes that facilitates creative problem solving and drives innovative solutions. Its customer-driven market focus ensures that solutions are sustainable and pragmatic. And that sustained presence provides stability for communities by providing the dignity of a good day's work and the pride that comes with providing for one's family. Over the past fifteen years, we have dedicated our lives to testing our theory—and the results are clear. Those with the courage to step up can truly change the world.

ACKNOWLEDGMENTS

Serving for decades in societies ravaged by conflict and poverty, one encounters hardship, injustice, and man's inhumanity to man almost on a daily basis. This was more than counterbalanced by the kindness, enthusiasm, and support shown to us by the generations of Business on the Frontlines students, alumni, advisors, donors, partners and communities. Although far too numerous to mention individually, they know who they are and have our sincere thanks. Mike Nevens and Paul Purcell never ceased to encourage us, even in our darkest hours. The University of Notre Dame and University of Alberta have provided ongoing support. Our stellar editors, Lynn Freehill-Maye and Jenn Brown, made each draft of this manuscript that much better. Our patient editor, Emily Taber, guided this effort every step of the way.

We dedicate this work to our parents. Neither this book nor the entire Business on the Frontlines adventure would have been possible had they not constantly encouraged us to seek the very best in ourselves.

NOTES

Introduction

1. *Official Report of Debates of the Legislative Assembly* (July 5, 1993), *Hansard*, 11:21.

2. Aimee Pichhi, "Meet the 8 Men Who Are Wealthier Than Half the Globe," CBS News, January 17, 2017, www.cbsnews.com/media/meet-the-8-men-who-are-wealthier-than -half-the-globe-davos-world-economic-forum/.

3. J. Mair, M. Wolf, and C. Seelos, "Scaffolding: A Process of Transforming Patterns of Inequality in Small-Scale Societies," *Academy of Management Journal* 59, no. 6 (2016): 2021–2044.

4. V. O. Bartkus and E. Conlon, *Getting It Right* (New York: Jossey Bass, 2008).

5. Margaret Mead quoted in D. Keys, *Earth at Omega: Passage to Planetization* (Wellesley, MA: Branden, 1982), 111.

6. E. S. Block and V, O. Bartkus, "Learning to Serve: Delivering Partner Value through Service-Learning Projects," *Academy of Management Learning & Education* 18, no. 3 (2019): 361–387.

7. General Douglas MacArthur quote chiseled into the wall by the U-boat at the Museum of Science and Industry in Chicago, www.msichicago.org/explore/whats-here/tours -and-experiences/u-505-on-board-tour/.

8. C. Blattman, *Why We Fight: The Roots of War and the Paths to Peace* (New York: Penguin Random House, 2022).

9. I. Diedhiou and Z. Yang, "Senegal's Fisheries Policies: Evolution and Performance," *Ocean & Coastal Management* 165 (2018): 1–8.

10. Overfishing is only one of the reasons that piracy emerged in Somalia. U. R. Sumaila and M. Bawumia, "Fisheries, Ecosystem Justice and Piracy: A Case Study of Somalia," *Fisheries Research* 157 (2014): 154–163.

11. C. T. Cleveland and D. Egel, *An American Way of Irregular War: An Analytical Memoir* (RAND: Washington, DC, 2020).

Chapter 1: The Juice Is Worth the Squeeze

1. We use pseudonyms in place of the given names of our partners to protect their privacy.

2. "Ugandans Cite Brutality and Corruption among Police Failings," Afrobarometer, February 20, 2023, www.afrobarometer.org/articles/ugandans-cite-brutality-and-corruption-among-police-failings/.

3. Dwight D. Eisenhower Presidential Library, Museum, and Boyhood Home, National Archives, Washington, DC, www.eisenhowerlibrary.gov/eisenhowers/quotes.

4. We call the middlemen with guns men because we did not run into any women with guns, although they may exist.

5 C. Onyango-Obbo, "In Once-Dreaded North Uganda, Beauty Grows from the Horrors of Long War," *East African* (Nairobi), March 5, 2023, www.theeastafrican.co.ke/tea/news/east-africa/beauty-grows-from-horrors-of-uganda-long-war-4145712.

6. P. Collier, *The Bottom Billion: Why the Poorest Countries Are Failing and What Can Be Done About It* (Oxford University Press: New York, 2008).

7. T. L. Friedman, *The World Is Flat: A Brief History of the Twenty-First Century* (Macmillan: New York, 2005).

8. US currency unless otherwise noted. C. K. Prahalad, *The Fortune at the Bottom of the Pyramid* (Prentice Hall: Upper Saddle River, NJ, 2005).

9. China Foreign Direct Investment 1979–2023 (2023), Macrotrends, www.macrotrends.net/countries/CHN/china/foreign-direct-investment; India Foreign Direct Investment 1970–2023 (2023), Macrotrends, www.macrotrends.net/countries/IND/india/foreign-direct-investment.

10. K. Rogoff, "China's Diminishing Returns," *Project Syndicate*, October 31, 2022, www.project-syndicate.org/commentary/china-diminishing-returns-real-estate-housing-slowdown-by-kenneth-rogoff-2022-10.

11. Given the limitations of World Bank and other statistics, we have excluded urban populations from our calculations. Partly, this is because the emerging middle classes in low-, lower-middle-, and upper-middle-income countries reside overwhelmingly in the cities. That being said, we believe that the same frontline conditions apply to the populations living in urban slums; our calculations likely understate the frontline opportunity. Furthermore, as countries transition from war into the gray arena of post-conflict transformation, they would further increase frontline opportunities.

12. Although Chinese businesses can invest in both Russia and North Korea.

13. "Trillions-to-Be: The CEA's Is the Latest in a Long List of Assertions on the Indian Economy's Growth," *Wire*, January 13, 2023, https://thewire.in/economy/five-trillion-dollar-economy-india.

14. "World GDP, PPP (Current International$)," (2023), World Development Indicators Database, World Bank, Washington, DC, https://data.worldbank.org/indicator/NY.GDP.MKTP.PP.CD?name_desc=true.

15. Robert M. Solow, "A Contribution to the Theory of Economic Growth," *Quarterly Journal of Economics* 70, no. 1 (1956): 65–94; Solow, "Technical Change and the Aggregate Production Function," *Review of Economics and Statistics* 39, no. 3 (1957): 312–320.

16. D. A. John and R. B. Giridhara, "Lessons from the Aftermath of the Green Revolution on the Food System and Health," *Frontiers in Sustainable Food Systems* 5 (2021): 644559.

17. Paul Collier and Anthony J. Venables, "Managing the Exploitation of Natural Assets: Lessons for Low Income Countries," in *African Economic Research Conference Proceedings* (Nairobi: African Economic Research Consortium, 2008), 26.

18. To learn more about the discourse around sustainability in the mining industry, please see V. Rajaram, S. Dutta, and K. Parameswaran, eds., *Sustainable Mining Practices: A Global Perspective* (Oxford: Routledge, 2005).

19. A. Bhargava, D. T. Jamison, L. J. Lau, and C. J. Murray, "Modeling the Effects of Health on Economic Growth," *Journal of Health Economics* 2, no. 3 (2001): 423–440. R. J. Basso, "Economic Growth in a Cross Section of Countries." *Quarterly Journal of Economics* 106, no. 2 (1991): 407–443.

20. A vast amount of research in management has demonstrated the advantages that accrue to first movers. See, for example, M. B. Lieberman and D. B. Montgomery, "First-Mover Advantages," *Strategic Management Journal* 9, no. S1 (1988): 41–58.

21. National Bureau of Non-governmental Organizations, Updated National NGO Register, (Kampala: Government of Uganda, 2023), www.ngobureau.go.ug/~ngoburea/en/updated-national-ngo-register.

22. 91st Civil Affairs Battalion, Lineage and Honors, Department of the Army, 2010, https://history.army.mil/HTML/forcestruc/lineages/branches/civaf/0091cabn.htm.

23. G. Gueye, *The Farmer Entrepreneurship Program (FEP) Project Case Study: Bridging Farmers to the Jollibee Supply Chain Project* (Baltimore: Catholic Relief Services, 2020), www.crs.org/sites/default/files/tools-research/crs_fep_jollibee_case_study.pdf.

24 "Comfandi Family Compensation Fund Improves Lives of More Than 800 Colombian Farmers," *3BL* (Bogota), November 14, 2019, www.3blmedia.com/news/family-compensation-fund-improves-lives-more-800-colombian-farmers.

Chapter 2: Security is Not a Fixed Cost

1. Total foreign direct investment in Ghana in 2002 was US$59 million. "Foreign Direct Investment, Net Inflows (% of GDP)—Ghana," World Bank, https://data.worldbank.org/indicator/BX.KLT.DINV.WD.GD.ZS?locations=GH.

2. OECD/SWAC, *Borders and Conflicts in North and West Africa*, West African Studies (Paris: OECD, 2022), https://doi.org/10.1787/6da6d21e-en.

3. For an up-to-date comparison of crime statistics between the two cities, please see "Crime Comparison between Baghdad and San Pedro Sula," Nombeo, www.numbeo.com/crime/compare_cities.jsp?country1=Iraq&city1=Baghdad&country2=Honduras&city2=San+Pedro+Sula.

4. *Transnational Organized Crime in Central America and the Caribbean: A Threat Assessment*, (Vienna: United Nations Office on Drugs and Crime, 2012), www.unodc.org/documents/data-and-analysis/Studies/TOC_Central_America_and_the_Caribbean_english.pdf.

5. GE partners with hospitals in Honduras to supply equipment: "GE Triples Its Developing Health Program in Honduras" (press release), November 20, 2008, www.ge.com/news/press-releases/ge-triples-its-developing-health-globally-program-honduras.

6. *Honduras Events of 2020* (Washington, DC: Human Rights Watch, 2021).

7. V. O. Bartkus, "'Untapped Resources' for Building Security from the Ground Up," *Joint Force Quarterly* 93 (2019), https://ndupress.ndu.edu/JFQ/Joint-Force-Quarterly-93aspx.

8. *The Other Oil Price: The Problem with Palm Oil* (London: Global Counsel, 2015), www.global-counsel.com/sites/default/files/Global_Counsel_GCI_the_other_oil_price_palm_oil.pdf.

Chapter 3: Savvy Supply Chains

1. P. J. Van Asten, L. W. I. Wairegi, D. Mukasa, and N. O. Uringi, "Agronomic and Economic Benefits of Coffee-Banana Intercropping in Uganda's Smallholder Farming Systems," *Agricultural Systems* 104, no. 4 (2011): 326–334.

2. R. E. Coase, "The Nature of the Firm," *Economica* 4 (1937): 386–405.

3. T. J. Pettit, L. Keeley, K. Croxton, and J. Fickel, "The Evolution of Resilience in Supply Chain Management: A Retrospective on Ensuring Supply Chain Resilience," *Journal of Business Logistics* 40, no. 1 (2019): 55–65.

4. H. Ritchie and M. Roser, "Farm Size and Productivity," Our World in Data, 2022, https://ourworldindata.org/farm-size. *Farms and Land in Farms* (Washington, DC: US Department of Agriculture, 2021), www.nass.usda.gov/Publications/Todays_Reports/reports/fnlo0222.pdf.

5. Dole, "Our Operations," 2023, www.doleplc.com/our-business/our-operations.

6. Dole, "Our Operations."

7. Cargill, "Cargill Supply Chain Footprint," 2023, www.cargill.com/sustainability/palm-oil/cargill-supply-chain-footprint.

8. *Global Coffee Platform for a Sustainable Coffee World: 2022 Report*, (Geneva: Global Coffee Platform, 2022), www.globalcoffeeplatform.org.

9. "Our Responsibility Is to the Land and Its People," Green Mountain Coffee Roasters, 2022, www.gmcr.com/responsibility?cm_sp=navigation-_-globalnav-_-responsibility

10. V. M. Viana, *Sustainable Development in Practice: Lessons Learned from Amazonas*, no. 3 (London: IIED, 2010.)

11. *Working to Make the Amazon Worth More Standing Than Cut Down* (Notre Dame, IN: University of Notre Dame, 2017), https://fas-amazonia.org/publicacao/working-to-make-the-amazon-worth-more-standing-than-cut-down/.

12. V. O. Bartkus, W. Brooks, J. P. Kaboski, and C. Pelnik, "Big Fish in Thin Markets: Competing with the Middlemen to Increase Market Access in the Amazon," *Journal of Development Economics* 155 (2022): 102757.

13. *Solucoes Para a Sustenabilidade—Guarana* (Manaus, Brazil: Foundation for Amazonas Sustainability, 2022), https://fas-amazonia.org/novosite/wp-content/uploads/2022/02/solucoes-guarana.pdf.

14. "Fruits of the Rainforest in a Profitable Harvest," *Financial Times*, September 27, 2005, www.ft.com/content/c6e2e87a-2f79-11da-8b51-00000e2511c8.

15. *World Development Report 2008: Agriculture for Development* (Washington, DC: World Bank, 2008).

16. J. Fargione, J. Hill, D. Tilman, S. Polasky, and P. Hawthorne, "Land Clearing and the Biofuel Carbon Debt," *Science* 319, no. 1235 (2008); published online February 7, 2008, doi:10.1126/science.1152747.

17. H, Godfray, J. Charles, J. R. Beddington, I. R. Crute, L. Haddad, D. Lawrence, J. F. Muir, J. Pretty, S. Robinson, S. M. Thomas, and C. Toulmin, "Food Security: The Challenge of Feeding 9 Billion People," *Science* 327, no. 5967 (2010): 812–818.

Chapter 4: Partnerships Mitigate Risk

1. Julia Symmes Cobb, "Gold Diggers: Illegal Mining," Reuters, May 17, 2021, www.reuters.com/world/china/gold-diggers-illegal-mining-near-colombian-town-hits-zi-jin-output-2021-05-18/.

2. "Chinese Firm Buying Continental Gold," *Toronto Star*, December 2, 2019, www .thestar.com/business/chinese-firm-buying-continental-gold/article_3464af67-6c97-5866 -9e18-05c1e0e00a8f.html.

3. Discontinuation of the tripartite economic and security program in Buritica was confirmed by the Colombian peace-building NGO to the authors.

4. Luis Jaime Acosta, "Operation at Zijin Colombia Mine Partially Halted After Attacks," Reuters, June 2, 2023, www.reuters.com/world/americas/operations -zijin-colombia-mine-partially-halted-after-attacks-2023-06-02/.

5. M. Bratton, "The Politics of Government-NGO Relations in Africa," *World Development* 17, no. 4 (1989): 569–587.

6. H. R. Clinton, *Hard Choices* (New York: Simon & Schuster, 2014).

7. S. A. Alvarez, J. B. Barney, and P. Anderson, "Forming and Exploiting Opportunities: The Implications of Discovery and Creation Processes for Entrepreneurial and Organizational Research," *Organization Science* 24, no. 1 (2013): 301–317.

8. V. O. Bartkus, "'Untapped Resources' for Building Security from the Ground Up," *Joint Force Quarterly* 93 (2019), https://ndupress.ndu.edu/JFQ/Joint-Force-Quarterly-93. aspx.

9. "Civil-Military Cooperation (CIMIC)," North Atlantic Treaty Organization, January 4, 2011, https://www.nato.int/cps/en/natohq/topics_69722.htm; Gilles Bergner, "A Presentation of CIMIC," *SFOR Informer Online*, www.nato.int/sfor/cimic/introduction/cimic.htm.

10. D. Kilcullen, *Out of the Mountains: The Coming Age of the Urban Guerrilla* (Oxford: Oxford University Press, 2015).

11. R. R. Ongsotto and R. Ongsotto, *Philippine History* (Manila: Rex, 2002).

12. F. Whaley, "Philippines and Rebels Agree on Peace Accord to End Insurgency," *New York Times*, January 26, 2014, www.nytimes.com/2014/01/26/world/asia/philippines -and-rebels-agree-on-peace-accord-to-end-insurgency.html.

13. "Gross Regional Domestic Product," Republic of Philippines—Philippine Statistics Authority, 2022, https://psa.gov.ph/statistics/grdp.

14. For a good review of sampling strategies, see O. C. Robinson, "Sampling in Interview-Based Qualitative Research: A Theoretical and Practical Guide," *Qualitative Research in Psychology* , no. 1 (2014): 25–41.

15. D. Moyo, *Dead Aid* (New York: Farrar, Straus and Giroux, 2009), 155.

Chapter 5: Follow the Money

1. "UNODC Report on Human Trafficking Exposes Modern Form of Slavery," United Nations Office on Drugs and Crime, 2008, www.unodc.org/unodc/en/human-trafficking/global-report-on-trafficking-in-persons.html.

2. *National Baseline Study on Violence against Children in the Philippines* (Manila: UNICEF, 2010), www.unicef.org/philippines/reports/national-baseline-study-violence-against-children-philippines.

3. "Who We Are," World Vision, 2023, www.worldvision.org.ph/about-us/.

4. "Philippines GDP per Capita 1960–2023," Macrotrends, 2023, www.macrotrends.net/countries/PHL/philippines/gdp-per-capita.

5. A. Hundschell, S, Razinskas, J. Backmann, and M. Hoegl, "The Effects of Diversity on Creativity: A Literature Review and Synthesis," *Applied Psychology* 71, no. 4 (2022); 1598–1634.

6. We borrow from Quinetta Roberson and colleagues' firm-level research on diversity as a dynamic capability. Q. Roberson, O. Holmes IV, and J. L. Perry, "Transforming Research on Diversity and Firm Performance: A Dynamic Capabilities Perspective," *Academy of Management Annals* 11, no. 1 (2017): 189–216.

7. This point is called "theoretical saturation" in grounded theory and occurs when "no new or relevant data seem to emerge in a category, the category is well developed in terms of its properties and dimensions demonstrating variation, and the relationships among categories are well established and validated." For more information, please see A. Strauss and J. Corbin, *Basics of Qualitative Research Techniques* (Thousand Oaks, CA: Sage, 1998), 212.

8. M. D'Silva and S. Imamović, *Resolving Protracted Displacement Through Social Housing* (Baltimore: Catholic Relief Services, 2015), www.fmreview.org/sites/fmr/files/FMR downloads/en/dayton20/dsilva-imamovic.pdf.

Chapter 6: Partner Broadly

1. Avi Kober, "The Israel Defense Forces in the Second Lebanon War: Why the Poor Performance?," *Journal of Strategic Studies* 31, no. 1 (2008): 3–40, www.tandfonline.com/doi/full/10.1080/01402390701785211.

2. K. Robinson, *What Is Hezbollah?* (Washington, DC: Council on Foreign Relations, 2022), www.cfr.org/backgrounder/what-hezbollah.

3. UN Human Rights Office of the High Commissioner, "Human Rights Council Discusses Report of Commission of Inquiry on Lebanon" (press release), December 1, 2006, www.ohchr.org/en/press-releases/2009/10/human-rights-council-discusses-report-commission-inquiry-lebanon.

4. Lebanon (profile), Observation of Economic Complexity, MIT, 2022, https://oec.world/en/profile/country/lbn.

5. "After Lebanon War Devastation, Hezbollah Suburb Now Booming," *Haaretz*, October 23, 2009, www.haaretz.com/2009-10-23/ty-article/after-lebanon-war-devastation-hezbollah-suburb-now-booming/0000017f-f8bf-d318-afff-fbff223c0000.

6. Hezbollah International Financing Prevention Act of 2015, H.R. 2297, 114th Cong. (2015), www.congress.gov/bill/114th-congress/house-bill/2297/text.

7.   P. Ellis, "Social Ties and Foreign Market Entry," *Journal of International Business Studies* 31, no. 3 (2000): 443–469; D. Morschett, H. Schramm-Klein, and B. Swoboda, "Decades of Research on Market Entry Modes: What Do We Really Know About External Antecedents of Entry Mode Choice?," *Journal of International Business Studies* 16, no. 1 (2010): 60–77.

8.   "Powering Africa's Human Capital Development: The Correlation Between Energy and Education," Energy Capital & Power, August 31, 2021, https://energycapitalpower.com /powering-africas-human-capital-development-the-correlation-between-energy-and-education/.

9.   Details of the legal requirements for electricity production can be found through the website of the Ugandan Electricity Regulatory Authority, www.era.go.ug/index.php/resource -centre/regulatory-instruments/laws.

10.   M. Lacey, "A Decade After Massacres, Rwandan Government Outlaws Ethnicity," *New York Times*, April 9, 2004, www.nytimes.com/2004/04/09/world/a-decade-after -massacres-rwanda-outlaws-ethnicity.html.

11.   J. D. Sachs, *The End of Poverty: Economic Possibilities for Our Time* (New York: Penguin Books, 2005).

12.   N. Munk, *The Idealist: Jeffrey Sachs and the Quest to End Poverty* (New York: Penguin Random House, 2013).

13.   A. Parmigiani and M. Rivera-Santos, "Clearing a Path Through the Forest: A Meta-review of Interorganizational Relationships," *Journal of Management* 37, no. 4 (2011): 1108 –1136.

Chapter 7: Imagine and Create Common Ground

1.   "Launch of Key Findings of Viet Nam's First Large-Scale National Survey on People with Disabilities (2016)" (press release), UNICEF, www.unicef.org/vietnam/press-releases/ launch-key-findings-viet-nams-first-large-scale-national-survey-people-disabilities.

2.   Since the war ended in 1975 more than forty thousand Vietnamese have been killed and another sixty thousand maimed by the land mines, artillery shells, and cluster bombs that had been left unexploded.

3.   K. Jehn, G. Northcraft, and M. Neale, "Why Differences Make a Difference: A Field Study of Diversity, Conflict and Performance in Workgroups," *Administrative Science Quarterly* 44 (1999): 4.

4.   E. Kapsetin and R. Kim, *The Socio-economic Impact of Newmont Ghana Gold Ltd.* (Haarlem, Netherlands: Stratcomm Africa, 2011), http://s24.q4cdn.com/382246808/files/ doc_downloads/operations_projects/africa/documents/Socio_Economic_Impact_of_ Newmont_Ghana_Gold_July_2011_0_0.pdf.

5.   The four commands were US Army Special Operations Command, 7th Special Forces Group, US Southern Command, and the Theatre Special Operations Command–South.dp.

6.   D. Moyo, *Dead Aid: Why Aid Is Not Working and How There Is a Better Way for Africa* (New York: Farrar, Straus and Giroux, 2009).

7.   *The Confessions of Saint Augustine* (397 CE), trans. F. J. Sheed (Cambridge: Hackett, 2006).

Chapter 8: Dirty Boots and Open Hearts

1. Bahasa Indonesia literally translates to "Indonesian language."

2. "Introduction: Cambodia 1975–1979," United States Holocaust Museum, 2018, www.ushmm.org/genocide-prevention/countries/cambodia/case-study/introduction/cambodia-1975.

3. 2010 Cambodia Demographic Health Survey (fact sheet), National Institute of Statistics, Directorate General for Health, 2010, www.dhsprogram.com/pubs/pdf/GF2 2/GF22.pdf.

4. A. M. Leung, L. E. Braverman, and E. N. Pearce, "History of U.S. Iodine Fortification and Supplementation," *Nutrients* 4, no. 11 (2012):1740–1746. doi: 10.3390/nu4111740 . Erratum in *Nutrients* 9, no. 9 (September 5, 2017): PMID: 23201844, PMCID: PMC3509517.

Chapter 9: Fail Fast and Fail Forward

1. "Under Five Mortality," UNICEF, 2023, https://data.unicef.org/topic/child-survival/under-five-mortality/.

2. CIA, "Obesity—Adult Prevalence Rate," *The World Factbook*, 2023, www.cia.gov/the-world-factbook/field/obesity-adult-prevalence-rate/country-comparison.

3. This deductive problem-solving framework is articulated fully in V. O. Bartkus and E. Conlon, *Getting It Right* (New York: Jossey Bass, 2008).

4. F. L. Dyer and T. C. Martin, *Edison: His Life and Inventions* (New York: Timeless Classic Books, 1910).

5. *Honduras: Strong Action Needed on Corruption* (Washington, DC: Human Rights Watch, 2023).

6. J. S. Hammond, R. L. Keeney, and H. Raiffa, "The Hidden Traps in Decision Making," *Harvard Business Review*, September–October 1998, https://hbr.org/1998/09/the-hidden-traps-in-decision-making-2.

Conclusion: Nothing Stops a Bullet Like a Job

1. COVID Response from the Janssen Pharmaceutical Companies of Johnson & Johnson, www.janssen.com/covid19.

2. COVID-19 Vaccine Tracker and Landscape, World Health Organization, 2023, www.who.int/teams/blueprint/covid-19/covid-19-vaccine-tracker-and-landscape; COVID19 Vaccine Tracker, December 2, 2022, https://covid19.trackvaccines.org/vaccines/1/.

3. R. Zimlich and M. Menna, (2023), "An Overview of the J&J COVID-19 Vaccine," Verywell Health, June 8, 2023, www.verywellhealth.com/johnson-and-johnson-covid-19-vaccine-5093160.

4. J. Wernau "Johnson & Johnson's Covid-19 Vaccine Emerges as Preferred Shot for Homeless," *Wall Street Journal*, April 4, 2021, https://www.wsj.com/articles/johnson-johnsons-covid-19-vaccine-emerges-as-preferred-shot-for-homeless-11617530400;N.Rattner, "J&J Vaccine Pause Makes It Tougher to Immunize Hard-to-Reach Populations Against COVID," CNBC, www.cnbc.com/2021/04/17/jj-vaccine-pause-could-make-it-harder-for-some-groups-to-get-a-shot.html.

5. "FDA Authorizes Johnson & Johnson's One-Shot COVID-19 Vaccine," National Public Radio, February 27, 2021, www.npr.org/sections/coronavirus-live-updates/2021/02/27/972009978/fda-authorizes-johnson-johnsons-one-shot-covid-19-vaccine.

6. "The Untreated Syphilis Study at Tuskegee Timeline," Centers for Disease Control and Prevention, 2022, www.cdc.gov/tuskegee/timeline.htm.

7. B. R. Kennedy, C. C. Mathis, and A. K. Woods, "African Americans and Their Distrust of the Health Care System: Healthcare for Diverse Populations," *Journal of Cultural Diversity* 14, no. 2 (2007).

8. A. M. Koskan, I. E. Lococo, C. L. Daniel, and B. S. Teeter, "Rural Americans' COVID-19 Vaccine Perceptions and Willingness to Vaccinate Against COVID-19 with Their Community Pharmacists: An Exploratory Study," *Vaccines* 11(1): 171.

9. Z. Abuza and L. Lischin, *The Challenges Facing the Philippines' Bangsamoro Autonomous Region* (Washington, DC: United States Institute for Peace, 2020), www.usip.org/sites/default/files/2020-06/20200610-sr_468-the_challenges_facing_the_philippines_bangsamoro_autonomous_region_at_one_year-sr.pdf.

10. P. Talhimhas, D. Batista, I. Diniz, and A. Vieira, "The Coffee Leaf Rust Pathogen *Hemileia vastatrix*: One and a Half Centuries Around the Tropics; Coffee Leaf Rust Caused by *Hemileia vastatrix*," *Molecular Plant Pathology* 18, no. 8 (2016): 1039–1051.

11. Robert D. Putnam, *Bowling Alone: The Collapse and Revival of American Community* (New York: Simon & Schuster, 2000).

12. J. P. Lederach, *The Moral Imagination: The Art and Soul of Building Peace* (Oxford: Oxford University Press, 2005), 5.

Viva Ona Bartkus is Paul E. Purcell Associate Professor of Management at the University of Notre Dame's Mendoza College of Business. She is a former partner at McKinsey & Company and the founder of the revolutionary Business on the Frontlines program.

Emily S. Block is the George M. Cormie Chair of Management in the University of Alberta School of Business. A former consultant for Accenture, Block now teaches negotiations and decision making and runs the university's Business on the Frontiers program.